Monica Swanson helps parents over[come] ... their children with confidence. *Bec[oming]* ... vational guide full of revolutionary insights and practical tools to homeschool well.

Ginger Hubbard, bestselling author, *Don't Make Me Count to Three* and *I Can't Believe You Just Said That*; podcast cohost, *Parenting with Ginger Hubbard*

Homeschooling is the best decision our family has made. I thought about writing a homeschooling book, but I don't have to; Monica wrote everything I would have said. Simply cannot recommend enough. Buy it. Read it all.

Jessica Smartt, author, *Memory-Making Mom* and *Let Them Be Kids*

Monica is offering exactly the wisdom and encouragement so many are looking for. And the best part: it's *joyful*. Reading this is like spending time with a friend who makes you feel more energized about what you're doing. This book will be a blessing to a lot of families.

Brant Hansen, author; radio host; dad of homeschooled kids; host, the *Brant and Sherri Oddcast* podcast

Homeschooling has been one of the most joyful, fulfilling experiences of my life. I deeply regret that I didn't do it sooner—but perhaps I would have if someone had given me a resource like this! *Becoming Homeschoolers* is the perfect introductory guide to what parents need to know. It's just the right mix of big-picture and detailed information that you need to start (and continue) your journey.

Natasha Crain, speaker; podcaster; author of four books, including *Faithfully Different*

By sharing her experience and wisdom as a veteran homeschooling mom, Monica clears the fog that many parents may experience as they consider homeschooling their children. She helps them prioritize, simplify, and begin to see how doable homeschooling really is. After homeschooling my own eight kids over the last thirty years, I can't recommend *Becoming Homeschoolers* highly enough!

Durenda Wilson, author, *The Unhurried Homeschooler*, *The Four-Hour School Day*, and *Raising Boys to Men*; host, *The Durenda Wilson Podcast*

Monica is sharing with the world her homeschooling experience and its impact in raising her *amazing* young men, and clearly she should be acknowledged as a hands-on pioneer and expert in her field. Monica isn't merely a researcher sharing her findings. She has lived this journey! She knows what she is talking about. Anyone interested in moving into the homeschooling realm, or already has jumped into it, would benefit greatly by gleaning from Monica's insights.

D. Melissa Brown, author; speaker; founder, Lifeways4living.com; homeschooling mom of seven incredible humans

Monica's newest book provides a clear, organized, delightful overview of most everything you'd need to know to step on and stay on—joyfully—the homeschool trail. With insight and humor she provides the real reasons to educate your children at home, as well as practical tips that will help you navigate through changes and challenges as your children grow through different stages. This is not just a read-it-once book but an I'll-visit-this-every-couple-of-years kind of book. Get it. Buy it. Read it.

Andrew Pudewa, founder and director, Institute for Excellence in Writing (IEW)

As a second-generation homeschooler, I've read a lot of homeschool books. *Becoming Homeschoolers* stands out from the crowd. Reading Monica's words felt like sitting down with a friend for coffee as she shared with me what a typical homeschool day looks like, answered questions about teaching my preschooler or preparing my teen for college, and most of all, helped me believe in the value and beauty of homeschooling. Wherever you are in your homeschooling journey, you'll find the wisdom, encouragement, and practical advice you need in *Becoming Homeschoolers*.

Greta Eskridge, second-generation homeschooler; author, *Adventuring Together* and *100 Days of Adventure*

Monica Swanson has uniquely captured the essence and motivation of homeschooling that allowed us to enjoy our kids and to create a culture our family has loved. We homeschooled all seven of our children. Our kids are all grown now, and after all these years, I wondered how there could be yet another book on why to homeschool, but *Becoming*

*Homeschoolers* is definitely different. This book will keep you inspired to live life to the fullest, with adventure, flexibility, joy, and vision. If you're considering homeschooling, *Becoming Homeschoolers* will help you work through the mindsets and reasons to go for it. We did it, and you can do it too.

Ann Dunagan, author, *Mission-Minded Families*

Monica's gone-before wisdom is a balm for the anxious homeschooling mom's heart. This book combines practical answers to questions every homeschooling (or would-be homeschooling) mom wants to know with can-do encouragement rooted in God's Word.

Abbie Halberstadt, author, *M Is for Mama*

Like a lot of families, we were thrust into homeschooling during the pandemic. We're still grateful we made that decision, but can I be honest? We weren't ready. I wish we would have had this excellent book to guide us. It's a gold mine of wisdom that will equip you to homeschool at every stage.

Drew Dyck, author, *Your Future Self Will Thank You* and *Just Show Up*

# BECOMING HOMESCHOOLERS

## GIVE YOUR KIDS A GREAT EDUCATION, A STRONG FAMILY, AND A LIFE THEY'LL THANK YOU FOR LATER

### MONICA SWANSON

ZONDERVAN BOOKS

ZONDERVAN BOOKS

Library of Congress Cataloging-in-Publication Data
Names: Swanson, Monica, author.
Title: Becoming homeschoolers : give your kids a great education, a strong family, and a life they'll thank you for later / Monica Swanson.
Description: Grand Rapids, MI : Zondervan, 2024.
Identifiers: LCCN 2023050816 (print) | LCCN 2023050817 (ebook) | ISBN 9780310367628 (trade paperback) | ISBN 9780310367635 (ebook)
Subjects: LCSH: Home schooling. | Home schooling—Religious aspects—Christianity. | Christian education— Home training. | Education—Parent participation. | Parent and child—Religious aspects—Christianity. | BISAC: EDUCATION / Home Schooling | RELIGION / Christian Living / Parenting
Classification: LCC LC40 .S94 2024 (print) | LCC LC40 (ebook) | DDC 371.04/2—dc23/eng/20240110
LC record available at https://lccn.loc.gov/2023050816
LC ebook record available at https://lccn.loc.gov/2023050817

*To the courageous parents who have homeschooled
throughout history. I am so grateful for the
path you have paved for the rest of us.*

---

*And to all of those who are choosing to homeschool
now and in the years to come. Your commitment
and sacrifice will impact your families and
the world in eternally significant ways.*

# CONTENTS

# FOREWORD

It's 1:35 p.m. My three "littles" are down for naps, and my four "olders" are playing games and running around outside. I'm pretty sure they took their metal detector and are finding treasures together. At any given moment I'm bound to hear the door burst open and a bunch of voices in unison saying, "Mom, look what we found!" or "You will never believe this!" while also clamoring for a snack.

They finished school around 11:30 a.m. today—right in time for lunch, which is what I usually aim for. I say "usually" because every day is different, and we have flexibility. "What a gift," I keep thinking. That thought has been in my head for six years now, but it settles deeper within me with each year of our homeschooling journey. What first felt daunting now feels more comfortable. I remember the night before my oldest started first grade. I was reading over my teacher manual, and it suddenly became overwhelming. I looked at my husband, slightly panicked, and said, "Babe, we aren't in kindergarten anymore." But after we completed that first week, I realized it wasn't what my fears had made it out to be. It was still fun. And guess what? The fun continues!

Years later I can now keep us on pace and organized but also know when we need to switch things up in our days or change how we organize our weeks and work together. Ahh, flexibility. It's my favorite word for our family and one good gift of homeschooling. I could list so many more homeschooling favorites, but luckily, as you turn these next pages, you'll quickly find that Monica has already done that. This entire book is a gift to the homeschooling world. What she shares is offered in such an encouraging and effectively loving way. She nails it (over and over again).

And that's Monica to a T. I've been on the encouraging end of her texts, emails, talks, and books. And, whew! You are in for a treat if you haven't experienced that before. This book is well worth your time. And not just because of Monica's kindness and natural ability to share her life and wisdom with those of us who need it (that's a bonus!). But also because of her ability to tackle a topic in such a compelling way that will have you walking away feeling built up and ready to take on the task and gift that is homeschooling.

I'm laughing to myself because I'm barely knee-deep in homeschooling and have learned so much, but I still have so much to learn. But you know what? I'm excited. Because the more I read *Becoming Homeschoolers*, the more I gleaned from Monica. It's like having the benefit of a close friend who walked out a whole path ahead of me and is now gracefully and *fully* sharing all her secrets and wisdom and learning with me because she cares for me. Yes. That's what this book is. And that's who Monica is.

I don't know what I anticipated when we started homeschooling. Whatever I thought I would get, "I got a lot of other things," as Monica says. I feel that sentiment deeply. There are so many things homeschooling is and will be for us. So many unexpected joys in the journey. As you dip your toes into this world of homeschooling, a world that may initially bring fears and doubts, I believe those will be quickly replaced by joys and shouts. Because with this journey, you'll get a lot of other (really *great*) things you didn't expect!

What an opportunity we have and what a gift it is. I truly believe that homeschooling allows us to pour into our kids the foundations and values of who God calls them to be, which is a clear way of directing them onto the right path, just as Proverbs 22:6 encourages: "Direct your children onto the right path, and when they are older, they will not leave it" (NLT). Another passage I love is Deuteronomy 6:6–7. God had just given the Ten Commandments to Moses and says, "You must commit yourselves wholeheartedly to these commands that I am giving you today. Repeat them again and again to your children. Talk about them when you are at home and when you are on the road, when you are going to bed and when you are getting up" (NLT). Wow! These are solid biblical encouragements that (1) align with our God-given mission as parents and (2) spur us on and motivate our homeschooling journey.

As you consider or continue homeschooling, trust that God will not only give you the wisdom you need each day but also bring people alongside you—people like Monica, who not only loves the Lord with her whole heart but also, practically speaking, can help guide and encourage you with her knowledge from walking the same road. I know I will keep this homeschooling guidebook forever (or at least for the next eighteen years) stacked on the top of my desk to flip through as often as needed. You'll want to reference it often to remind and encourage yourself why you are homeschooling. Whether it's through statistics, studies, or the personal stories Monica shares, this book offers what we all need. Monica paves a doable path.

Moms, this book is for you! Dads, this book is for you too! Monica wrote this in a way that will be most effective for families and parents who are making big decisions about their children's education in every season. Even if dads aren't the ones staying home and doing the bulk of the teaching, their role is invaluable, and in these pages they will find wisdom on how to support and engage.

My second grader is currently learning about imperative sentences, so here is one for you: Read every page of this book, and then once you do, don't be afraid to read it again a year later. And then pass it around to your husband, friends, neighbors, and whoever else needs it. Just make sure they give it back and get their own copy. It's too valuable to lose.

It's obvious this book has been prayed over and passionately written to give strength to those of us choosing the homeschool path. Because we are all in it together. What a gift that is!

Sarah Molitor, creator of Modern Farmhouse
Family and author of *Well Said*

# A WELCOME NOTE

Aloha! And welcome to *Becoming Homeschoolers*.

I'm guessing many of you would say that just a couple of years ago, you never would have imagined picking up a book with the word *homeschool* in the title. I get that, because a younger Monica would be most surprised of all that one day she would be authoring a book like this. Homeschooling was not even on my radar twenty-four years ago when I started parenting.

*But here we are.* Me writing this book, and you reading it. I consider it an honor to get to share our family's journey with you, as well as stories from other homeschooling families. Besides giving you helpful information and encouraging you, I really hope to become friends through the pages of this book. Whatever you end up doing for your kids' education, know that I am cheering for you to give them the very best you have.

There are a lot of good reasons to consider homeschooling, and I'm hoping to shine a light on many of them in this book. I also think we can agree that our world has been undergoing a lot of change in the past few years (#understatement). As intentional parents, we want to navigate our children's education with eyes wide open. I guess that's why we're both here.

I want to be clear that it is not my intent to bash the public school system here or suggest that there is only one right way to educate your kids. While I am saddened by many of the things going on in America's public schools, I also know there are teachers and administrators in all kinds of schools who are working hard to protect kids and trying to steer the ship in the right direction. I am very grateful for them. I am also aware that each of our life situations is unique and

> Our world has been undergoing a lot of change in the past few years (#understatement). As intentional parents, we want to navigate our children's education with eyes wide open.

that the educational choices we make for our kids are impacted by many factors. How we each navigate our kids' education requires an abundance of grace.

But when all is said and done, as parents we are responsible for the upbringing of our own children—and school is a big part of that. If you're already homeschooling, I hope this book offers you a ton of affirmation and some new ideas and practical help. If you're considering homeschooling, I hope this book provides you with enough information and encouragement to nudge you off that fence to begin your homeschool journey.

If you're still uncertain and not entirely convinced that homeschooling could be the best choice for your family, here's a short quiz to help you decide if homeschooling might be a good option for you and your kids. Just answer yes or no to the following statements:

1. I am curious about what it would look like to homeschool my kids.
2. I want to choose what my kids are learning.
3. I want to spend as much time as possible with my kids while they are growing up.
4. I believe my child has special gifts or special needs that would best be served by a custom home education.

5. I am concerned about bullying in schools.

6. I worry about school violence.

7. Our family wants to travel or do school on our own schedule.

8. I love to teach and love the idea of teaching my own kids.

9. I love to learn and love the idea of learning alongside my kids.

10. I want my kids to grow up having close relationships with each other.

11. My child is interested in pursuing a sport or extracurricular activity that would be best supported through a home education.

12. I want my kids to experience a well-rounded education with opportunities to learn things outside of a typical classroom setting.

13. I want faith to be an integral part of my child's education.

14. I don't want my child to waste hours of their day standing in lines, waiting for kids who misbehave, or doing unessential busywork.

15. I want to be the one to teach my child about sexuality and gender.

16. I do not want my child to be taught a purely evolutionary view of creation.

17. I want to protect my child from being confused by an administration, teachers, or students who want to push a cultural or social agenda that does not align with our family values.

18. I don't like rushing to get out the door every morning.

19. I don't like unnecessary homework.

20. I just really like my kids a lot.

If you answered yes to *any* of the statements above, then *yes*, you will benefit from what we are about to cover in this book, and homeschooling may be a great fit for your family.

My hope is that *Becoming Homeschoolers* will be a guidebook for you—a favorite resource you will hold on to and return to as your child hits various ages and stages. I like to imagine that it will be dog-eared and scribbled on and worn out over the years. Each chapter is packed with personal stories, practical advice, and helpful information, and still I wish I could have added even more. I should also note here: With our world changing at lightning speed, I'm aware that soon after this book comes out there are likely to be new issues, curriculums, and topics that I will wish I could have covered. Yet I always say that wisdom principles are timeless, so I do hope that the things we cover in this book will be relevant to even any unforeseen changes ahead!

God's Word has been the foundation for our family and our homeschool journey, so you will find Bible verses and mentions of my faith throughout this book. However, regardless of your faith, I hope you feel welcome here. I believe that everyone who is interested in homeschooling will find practical help and encouragement in the pages ahead.

Be sure to check out the resource list at the end of this book. I worked hard to gather the best books, websites, and other resources and put them all in one place for you. It's one of my favorite parts of the book and I think you'll find it super helpful!

Finally: You can find me blogging and podcasting at my home base: monicaswanson.com. I love to get to know my readers, so please make yourself at home there and jot me a note as you read to tell me what you think. I read every email: aloha@monicaswanson.com.

Now grab your coffee, tea, or kombucha, and let's begin this adventure!

# HOW WE BECAME HOMESCHOOLERS

## (And Why It's Been the Best Decision for Our Family)

I remember the day like it was yesterday: I was working furiously on the final chapter of my previous book, *Raising Amazing*. I sat at my desktop computer, steaming latte sitting on the desk next to me, and my husband, a medical doctor, sat working on his laptop on our bed—his usual place to work on hospital notes. I had come to the chapter of the book titled "How They Spend Their Days," where I emphasized the importance of being intentional about the people, environment, and influences that shape our kids' days as they grow up.

I had just read a statistic—and I did the math myself to confirm it—that kids who go to a traditional school spend more than fourteen thousand hours of their growing-up years in school. *Fourteen thousand hours!* My heart rate jumped when I saw that number. That's more of their waking hours than they would spend anywhere else—including at home.

I already knew I wanted to spend a brief part of *Raising*

*Amazing* sharing about our family's own homeschool experience and encouraging readers to consider the many benefits of homeschooling their own kids. But the brief paragraph I had outlined on the topic soon spilled over into another and another, until I had pages filled with writing about homeschooling.

I laugh now, imagining myself that day like a cartoon character with smoke rising from my computer as my fingers flew across the keyboard. Fully absorbed in my writing, I hardly heard my husband's voice. When he repeated himself, I finally lifted my head just enough to see him watching me and smiling.

"Passionate about something over there?" he asked.

I let out a sigh, shook my head slowly, and confessed, "I don't think I've been totally honest."

"What do you mean?" Dave asked, seeming concerned.

"Well, I've written two parenting books now, and I hope and pray they are helping parents to raise amazing kids, but..."

"But what?" Dave waited.

"I've talked about homeschooling before. I mean, I never shy away from talking about how great it has been *for our family*. It's not like I ever purposefully left things out."

"And...?" Dave pushed. (I could tell I was frustrating the man.)

"There's something I don't think I've ever admitted to myself or to anyone else," I said, pausing a moment before plunging ahead. "I'm pretty sure that the greatest factor in shaping our boys' lives, outside of their relationship with Jesus, has been that we homeschooled them. Homeschooling isn't just a nice little part of their growing-up story. *It's the main story.*"

> Homeschooling isn't just a nice little part of their growing-up story. *It's the main story.*

There. I'd said it. And everything in me knew it was true. Dave nodded his head in full agreement and simply said, "Then keep writing."

So I did.

The next week, I went back to that chapter with fresh eyes and cleaned it up a bit, cutting some of the extra-passionate parts before turning in the manuscript. When my book edits came back a few weeks later, my editor had cut even more of the homeschooling content. (As in, she suggested we cut *most* of it.) But in the sidebar of the manuscript, she wrote, "Maybe this is for your next book . . . a book about homeschooling." With a smiley face emoji.

I showed her note to my husband. We looked at each other and knew: it was time. Time to finally share this amazing part of our family's life with the world. With fingers free to fly across the keyboard and a big smile on my face, I dove back into my passion for homeschooling—the choice that has shaped so much of my children's lives. And I am excited now to get to share with you an entire book on this topic that's so close to my heart.

## How We Started

If you'd told Dave and me when we first married that we'd be homeschooling four children, we'd have labeled you crazy and quickly found somewhere else we needed to be. Homeschooling wasn't something we'd even discussed. Both of us grew up going to public schools in small towns in the Pacific Northwest. We met and married in our midtwenties, then spent four years in Portland, Oregon, where Dave was going to medical school. I had studied sports medicine in college, but while Dave was in medical school, I got my teacher credentials and taught in our local public school.

Our first son, Josiah, was born before Dave's final year of medical school. We then moved to Hawaii for his medical residency program just before Josiah turned two and our second son, Jonah, was born. By the time Dave's three-year residency program was over, we had three active young boys. Though our living situation was small and simple, we took advantage of a fenced-in yard and strolls to the park. Daily trips to the beach became our sanity savers. When Dave was offered a job at a local hospital, we decided to make Hawaii home. While I missed the Pacific Northwest (autumn! and family and friends . . .), we saw the warm, laid-back island lifestyle—along with the opportunity to spend a lot of time unplugged and in nature—as an incredibly healthy way to raise young boys.

Looking back, I don't remember talking about or even *thinking* a lot about schooling options for our kids in their early years. The fall before our third son, Luke, came along, we figured that our then-four-year-old, Josiah, could use a little mental stimulation. (Or maybe we wanted more socialization for him? Or perhaps the grandparents had suggested it?) So we signed him up for part-time preschool. The next year he moved on to kindergarten, and the year after that he went to first grade. His younger brother Jonah began preschool as well. I was home alone with our third son, Luke, when I finally started to dream about how my life would look when all three boys were in school. Yes, I was crazy about my boys, but they were loud and messy and full of energy. I fantasized about a few kid-free hours at home on a regular basis. Maybe lunch with a friend? (Or at least an uninterrupted trip to the bathroom?) I had put my time in with three boys back-to-back. Plus, I had never considered *not* sending them to school. It hadn't even crossed my mind.

Both Dave and I had grown up with moms who were full-time homemakers, and I loved having my mom there for me when I got out of school each day. I had always dreamed that one day my life might look a lot like my mom's. Mom grew beautiful flowers and baked fresh bread and did such a great job of keeping our home tidy and welcoming that I might have mistakenly thought her job was easy. (Now I know better.) I would smile to myself as I imagined welcoming Dave home from work to clean counters and a happy, rested wife.

I was also aware that with medical school loans hanging over our heads and the high cost of living in Hawaii, we could use some extra income. I even glamorized how that might look. (Maybe I'd dress up for work? And get my nails done?) Or, I remember dreaming, what if I could write a blog and find a way to work from home? I had plenty of ideas for how my life might look when the boys went off to school. But however it might look, I was convinced that my future was looking bright. And clean. And quiet.

So you can probably imagine my reaction when Josiah came home from first grade one day and, over apple juice and a granola bar, threw me this curveball: "Mom, would you homeschool me next year?"

*Wait. What?*

My eyes grew big and my heart hit an extra beat, but I laughed and smiled as I tried to brush it off as silly talk. "Homeschool? Why would you think of that? You are so smart, and you do great in school!"

He looked down, and I realized it wasn't silly talk to him. "Some of the kids in Sunday school are homeschooled. And they said it's really fun."

*Fun?* I thought. *For whom?*

My mind quickly swirled like the current in our ocean. Weren't homeschoolers a little . . . odd? I remembered a particular homeschooling family I'd known when I was growing up. They could have been the inspiration for a *Saturday Night Live* skit. The mom wore a denim jumper and had long, stringy hair. Not kidding. And the kids? They were all just a bit . . . *off*. Awkward. Extra pale. I hadn't thought of them in years, but they were the first image to pop into my mind at my son's mention of homeschooling.

"Hey, Josiah, why don't you go outside and play with your brothers before we have to go to soccer?" I suggested, hoping to end this conversation before it progressed any further.

Josiah obediently let it go and joined his brothers outside.

But *I* couldn't let it go. Later that night when Dave came home, I told him about Josiah's unexpected question.

Dave brushed it off. "Homeschool? Can you just do that . . . *like, legally*? I don't know—I think kids need to be around other kids. I don't think doing school at home would be a good idea. Plus, you're always burned-out on the kids. There's *no way* you could handle it."

*Ouch.* That one hurt, but he was right. If I couldn't keep it together from 7:00 to 8:00 a.m., when I was getting everyone ready for school, there was no way I could have my kids home with me all day.

Right?

Or could I?

I loved those boys so much. It hurt my heart to think of how much I loved them. Maybe I *could* homeschool them. But *how*? What do you teach a seven-year-old? *All day long?* Jonah wasn't even reading yet. There was no way I could teach a kid to read. *Could I?* Even with teaching credentials under my belt, teaching kids at home felt like an entirely different undertaking.

And homeschooling would make them strange, right? And me too? (The denim jumper look just wasn't my thing.)

Oh, and then there was college. I would never know how to prepare a kid for college. Never mind. This was all just *crazy talk*.

The anxious thoughts kept coming, though, one after the other after the other. Followed by questions. Fears. Doubts. But the idea wouldn't leave my mind, and gradually, over the next few weeks, those negative thoughts turned to curiosity. And, strangely enough, a bit of excitement began to creep in. Finally, I decided to at least pray about it. And I asked Dave to pray as well.

By the following fall, my two oldest sons were doing school at home—*with me.* (Son number three, Luke, had started pre-school but would eventually join us at home as well.) I still had a lot of questions and even more self-doubt. We didn't know what we were doing at the time, but now I know—we were *becoming homeschoolers.*

## Official Homeschoolers

More than seventeen years have passed since we began our home-school journey. After our initial decision to bring our kids home, we continued to homeschool all three boys, and then a few years later, we added another student to our "classroom"—our fourth son, Levi. The oldest three boys have all graduated from high school, and not one of them is awkward or extra pale. Josiah, the one who started it all, graduated from college, backpacked through Europe with a friend, secured a great job, and is now financially independent and busy adulting in Santa Barbara, California. (He's also one of my very best friends.)

Between that first day of considering homeschooling and today, all my questions were eventually answered. Not all at once, but a little at a time over time. I did teach my kids to read (it's not that hard), and I found out that "schoolwork" doesn't have to take all day. (In fact, it *shouldn't* take all day.) I found great resources to teach from, and when we came to subjects that were beyond me, we used online classes and co-ops. Along the way, we also found a great community to do life and school with. All my fears were put to rest.

Instead of being overwhelmed by the kids being at home all day, I was pleasantly surprised to find that homeschooling was *less* stressful than the one-hour morning rush to get ready for school. I didn't miss the homework battles (there was no more homework), paper signing, or lunch packing. Over time we found a natural rhythm to our days, and I experienced the joy of seeing my kids light up when they learned about the solar system or volcanoes or grasped tens and hundreds place value. (That last one was harder than I expected.) Snuggling up with the boys to read stories about explorers or missionaries became one of my favorite parts of the day (and theirs too, they tell me now). And I learned that while a homeschool classroom could include desks and chairs, it more often looked like the kitchen counter or a blanket in the grass or the back seat of the car as we headed to the beach for an afternoon surf with Dad.

Dave's homeschool skepticism faded, too, as he was able to spend more quality time with his boys and we were able to travel to see extended family when most kids were in school. Then he *really* became a fan of our homeschooling life when he saw the character of our boys developing free from the daily influence of other kids, teachers we didn't choose or agree with, and all the other "stuff" that goes on when your kids are away from you the majority of the day.

No, I never got my quiet home, and lunch with friends has required some strategic planning. But I got a lot of other things, including the peace of knowing I gave my boys an incredible gift with our homeschooling. I also learned to teach—and parent—with dignity and confidence. I realized that, alongside their dad and with God's help, I had what it takes to raise up these kids to become life-ready young adults. Sure, I did most of it in the comfort of sweatpants, not a cute business suit, but I'm pretty sure that was a win too.

And eventually I did start that blog. Which led to books and a podcast. All while continuing to homeschool. And, well, here I am, encouraging you to join me in this homeschool journey.

## Now More Than Ever

I realize our world has changed a lot since I started homeschooling my boys. Back when we first started homeschooling, I wasn't thinking about school shootings, worldwide pandemics, or the growing cultural tensions we have grown so familiar with. I would never have imagined a time when schools taught countless pronouns. I hadn't heard of social media, sexting, or cyberbullying. I started homeschooling simply because my son wanted to learn at home, with me. And I'm so grateful I did.

Yet the more recent changes in our culture and especially in the public schools have led to a dramatic rise in homeschooling. In fact, according to an analysis done by the *Washington Post*, homeschooling has become the "fastest-growing form of education in America. . . . The growth demonstrates home schooling's arrival as a mainstay of the American educational system, with its impact—on society, on public schools and, above all, on hundreds of thousands of children now learning outside a conventional academic setting—only beginning to be felt."[1]

Indeed, the time is right to consider homeschooling. So throughout the rest of this book, I will share with you the joys—and the realities—of our homeschooling adventure, as well as all the information you need for your own homeschool adventure. If you're even barely considering giving learning at home a try, I'm laying it all out for you here. (I see you, hesitant one, and I'm so glad you're here!)

This book is our real-life, honest story—from those scary and insecure beginnings to all our questions and concerns along the way. From the beauty of easy mornings to the reality of some really long days. *And weeks.* From worrying about socialization to realizing that *good* socialization is one of the greatest blessings of homeschooling. I'll share with you how we chose curriculum, as well as how our family navigated busy sports schedules, standardized testing, and college applications.

I'll tell you about the experience of my two older boys taking a gap year, followed by the process of applying for—and receiving—significant college scholarships. You'll learn about my third son, who is doing online college while traveling the world, surfing professionally. And you'll get to know Levi, who at thirteen is growing up in a very different world than his brothers knew at his age. I'll share a lot of other people's experiences, too, because there is no one right way to homeschool. Many creative folks are out there, providing their kids with a home-based education, whether the parents work inside or outside of the home. (Where there's a will, there's a way, and I have some great ideas for you.) We'll talk about the legal stuff, the fun stuff, and the highly academic stuff.

But more important than all that, I want to tell you about the relationship my husband and I have formed with our four sons and the friendships our kids have developed with one another. I want to tell you about how their faith grew daily as they learned through the lens of a biblical worldview. I'll share some sweet conversations we've had over midmorning breaks, during lunch-hour shenanigans, and while packing produce for the homeless at our local food bank. I'll tell you about family vacations we took in November and how we took "snow days" in Hawaii. I want to offer you a vision of kids exploring their passions, reading great books, and being free to be 100 percent themselves—in all their quirky, hilarious individuality. I want to encourage you to give your kids the kind of freedom that allows them to grow up to be authentically who God created them to be—away from the pressure to conform to the ever-moving target of cultural coolness.

> Give your kids the kind of freedom that allows them to grow up to be authentically who God created them to be—away from the pressure to conform to the ever-moving target of cultural coolness.

I'll never say that homeschooling is for everyone. I do, however, believe that a lot more people would do it—and love it—if they tried it . . . *really* tried it. (And for the record, homeschooling is nothing like pandemic distance learning.)

If you are already homeschooling, I hope you finish this book with a fresh appreciation and enthusiasm for the journey you are on, and maybe even a few new ideas or inspirations to add to your experience. If you read this and decide that homeschooling is not for you, I hope you still come away feeling inspired to be involved and invested in your kids' education and to make the most of your family time together. (I may be pro-homeschooling, but more than that I am pro-family.) But if reading this book gives you the nudge you need to go for it and give homeschooling a try, you've just made my whole year!

So let's dive in, shall we?

PART I

DECIDING TO HOMESCHOOL

## CHAPTER 1

# THE LIFE THEY'LL THANK YOU FOR LATER (PART 1)

## 20 Good Reasons to Homeschool Your Kids

"What has been your favorite part of homeschooling?"

That's a question I've been asked many times. And every time, my mind drifts back over a thousand memories. Though our homeschool experience was not all butterflies and rainbows (we had some hard days—and seasons), I'm so glad it's the sweet memories that come to me first . . .

Three little boys gathered around a big world map, shouting, "Look! There's the North Pole!" and "Our island looks so tiny out there in the middle of the ocean!"

All the boys gathered in the living room, listening to Dad or Mom read the Bible or a missionary story, followed by questions and conversation about what we read.

Middle school boys up at dawn, determined to get through two subjects (required by Mom) before heading out to spear fish with some of the young men in our church.

Teenage boys gathered for lunch at our kitchen counter, gobling up leftover spaghetti while swapping stories and laughs or debating current events.

Kids reading books under trees, snuggled up with the dog or in the back of the car headed to the beach.

And (how can I not mention?) December, when Christmastime is welcomed into our school days with hot cider and Christmas music and the boys work hard to hit the "halfway mark" in their classes so they might take an extra long break to enjoy the holidays (and the big winter surf).

How can you put these sorts of images into words that might answer the "favorite part of homeschooling" question? I don't think you can, so I often boil it down to something much too simple, like "Maybe the strong family relationships," or "Giving my boys a faith-centered education."

I also sometimes mention that when my kids finally did launch out of our home to go away to college, I honestly felt like *we were all ready*. We had spent such good years together that I wasn't holding on to my boys when it was time for their next season.

But perhaps the greatest takeaway from our family's homeschool journey has been the way my boys themselves reflect on their experiences. They each have told me that they loved their childhood deeply and wouldn't trade the life we gave them for anything. Of course there is no perfect childhood, but they are grateful for what they had. And thus far, all four of my boys say they plan to homeschool their own kids one day. I think that says a lot!

Every homeschool parent (and student) will have their own list of personal highlights, (and let's be honest—lowlights as well,) but the reasons to homeschool your kids are many! In fact, here's a top twenty list that touches on some of the best reasons I can think of to begin the journey of homeschooling.

## 1. Homeschooled Students Consistently Perform Above Average on Standardized Tests

Homeschoolers are known to be excellent learners, and statistics give evidence of this, with homeschooled students consistently posting above-average scores on standardized tests. These findings have been shown to be true for homeschooled students from families across the board, taking both socioeconomic and racial status into consideration. In an article reviewing years of research, Lisa Treleaven notes that "homeschooling is the only education approach in which youth of low SES [socioeconomic status] achieve at levels that are as high scholastically as those of their higher-SES counterparts."[1]

## 2. Homeschooled Students Are Increasingly Being Recruited by Colleges

Colleges have begun to recognize that homeschooled students are mature and responsible, that they pursue unique passions, and that they are self-directed learners. In an NBC News article titled "Colleges Welcome a Growing Number of Homeschool Students," Katie Fretwell, an Amherst College dean of admissions and financial aid, remarked that homeschooled students "tend to have 'thicker folders, in a good way'" and that they tend to be "innovative thinkers with a lot to bring to the table."[2]

For example, Olivia S. Farrar, a former student at Harvard, was homeschooled up until she went to college. In the *Harvard Crimson*, she claimed that "homeschooling prepared me for Harvard really well because it fostered such a strong love for the act of learning. Not learning for a grade, not learning for an exam, but learning for the sheer love of knowledge itself."[3]

## 3. Homeschooling Is Efficient and Allows Kids to Learn Time Management

A typical public school day contains much activity that is, without a doubt, a waste of time. Homeschooled kids get to skip standing in endless lines, waiting for teachers to help (or deal with) other students, doing boring busywork, and many other useless things. They can get the academic part of their day completed in a surprisingly short amount of time if they organize their time well. (And they also learn what it's like to drag things out for no good reason and miss out on the fun—just as my youngest son did this week.) Time management is an important life skill, and homeschoolers have a great opportunity to learn it early on. My college sons say that organizing their time in college has been very similar to their high school homeschooling experience. While many of their classmates struggled to make the adjustment, my boys eased right into the routine.

> Time management is an important life skill, and homeschoolers have a great opportunity to learn it early on.

## 4. Homeschooling Families Can Offer Gifted or Challenged Students a Specialized Education

Research done by the *Washington Post* has shown that one in three homeschool parents said that their concern over how schools served children with special needs prompted them to homeschool.[4]

Homeschooling gives you the freedom to move at just the right pace for your child. In some situations that means you get to accelerate the academics while at other times you will need to move more slowly through one or more subjects. Young kids who are ready for high level classes or want to dive deep into certain subjects can do so. Kids who meet with therapists or have any sort of special accommodations are free to follow a schedule that works best for them, and being at home can greatly streamline that process.

One of my friends has homeschooled her three kids, two of whom have ADHD and another who was born with significant medical issues. She recalls her kids doing school in doctor's office waiting rooms and in the car while waiting for appointments. Their family planned schoolwork around surgeries and recovery. Homeschooling has allowed this family to support their child's medical needs and to foster compassion, flexibility, and other important character traits in all of the kids.

## 5. Homeschooled Kids Can More Freely Pursue Their Passions and Interests

For kids who are passionate about music, sports, or other interests, homeschooling can be a huge benefit. They can practice or train at times that are best for them and can travel without worrying about school absences. Luke began to dedicate many hours a day to his surfing career during middle school, and being able to arrange his own schedule was a huge blessing. Now Levi is an avid golfer, and he enjoys the freedom to golf and to plan his schoolwork around the weather, his coaches, and all the other factors involved in sports. (You'll find more on sports in chapter 11.)

Even if kids don't yet have a specific passion or interest, homeschooling offers them a great opportunity to explore new things. By middle school, my older boys were learning photography, videography, and computer coding, along with teaching themselves to play guitar and piano. They dabbled in bird-watching and rock collecting, got involved in youth ministry, and tried out a variety of sports and hobbies, some of which they did not love but were glad they had the chance to try. Many of these hobbies and skills have stuck and continue to be a part of their well-rounded lives as young adults.

## 6. Homeschooled Students Are Prepared for the Real World

While doing school at home, kids observe their parents doing the things that adults do in real life. We pay bills, fix broken things (or find someone to fix them for us), plan the family calendar, and manage all the things that our children will one day have to do as well. Kids naturally ask questions, take notes, and often end up stepping in to help with normal tasks that are all a part of "adulting." Before our oldest son left for college, my husband and I were able to travel off the island, leaving him in charge of the house, the animals, and his younger brothers more than once, and he did a great job managing the responsibilities.

## 7. Homeschooling Fosters Strong Relationships between Kids and Parents

By far, one of the greatest blessings of homeschooling for me has been building relationships with my sons. I know my boys well, and they truly know me. We've done life together. We've started and ended our days together. We've wrestled with math problems and watched news events unfold in real time (and stopped to discuss and pray about those events). We've journeyed through great books, eaten a gazillion meals, and lived the good, the bad, and the everything-in-between days together. My boys respect me for showing up every day. They see and know all that I do in a day. (Parents, we do a lot!) And, in turn, I respect my boys because I see and know all that they do too.

I especially love that my boys have been able to spend a lot of time with their father. Homeschooling has allowed us to tailor their schooling around his sometimes-unpredictable hospital schedule. On his days off work, Dave has poured countless hours into taking the boys surfing or to the skate park, and I often scheduled my own appointments or errands around his time off, which gave him the chance to put on his teacher hat and cover some school subjects with them. A school lesson with Dad usually led to related dinner-time conversations and a deeper dive into each subject without the boys even realizing how much they were learning.

## 8. Homeschooled Kids Build Strong Bonds with Their Siblings

My four sons are best friends, and I am positive this has a lot to do with their homeschool experience. They didn't always get along perfectly (far from it at times), but as they spent most of their days together, they learned to work things out. The older boys helped the younger ones with math or writing assignments. They took some of their classes together, did chores together, and had snacks and lunches together. They played in the yard between classes together. They bonded through all these experiences, and to this day, they choose time together over time with anyone else. (Recently I overhead them discussing how they hope to all grow up to live—and raise families—within walking distance of one another.)

Even though our fourth son was born six and a half years after our third son, they value their sibling relationship so much that his older brothers have been intentional about including him and building strong relationships with him. The four of them have taken "brother road trips," and they all FaceTime each other often.

## 9. Homeschooling Allows Families to Travel and Do School around Their Unique Schedules

School can happen in a million different ways, and depending on your interests, lifestyle, and schedules as parents, you can take full advantage of this flexibility. Traveling from Hawaii is expensive, so being able to take trips during the offseason or when it works for our family has been super helpful. I have a friend who has homeschooled her three kids on the road for months at a time in an RV and across Europe with backpacks. School doesn't always have to happen during traditional school hours or certain calendar months.

## 10. Homeschooled Kids Have an Easier Time Getting Internships, Which Can Lead to Getting Jobs Later On

As soon as a child discovers an area of interest, they will likely be able to find a business that is more than happy to have them on board as an intern. I go into depth on this topic in chapter 10, including sharing about some of the things my boys did. (There's also a great list of internship ideas in the resource section at the back of the book.) All these experiences look excellent on college applications and résumés for future jobs.

## 11. Homeschooling Families Can Integrate Character Lessons into the Whole Day Every Day

If you have read my previous books or listened to my podcast, you know that I talk a lot about the importance of character development in our children. Good and godly character is so important for our kids' future success, yet they will be hard-pressed to see examples of it in our youth culture. It is our job as parents to teach and train our kids to develop noble character. I like how American ethnographer George A. Dorsey said it: "Good, honest, hardheaded character is a function of the home. If the proper seed is sown there and properly nourished for a few years, it will not be easy for that plant to be uprooted."[5]

If we hope to raise kids of character, we have our work cut out for us (though I believe it absolutely can be done). My online Character Training Course has helped families all over the world to embrace godly character, and I will keep cheering on families as long as I have breath. But there is no doubt: a homeschool lifestyle—one where character can be integrated into every subject—offers a huge leg up over a traditional school environment that often works against our efforts to nurture character in our kids. (Also: find out about my Character Training Course in the resource section.)

## 12. Homeschooled Kids Can Learn Everything through a Biblical Worldview

I love that my boys can see God's fingerprints in math and science, literature, and history. Josiah became fascinated with mathematical principles and loved discovering things like Fibonacci's number sequence in the details of plants or a whale's fin and throughout the design of our universe. History ("His story") comes to life when you learn through the lens of a biblical worldview. And choosing great books about heroes of the faith over some questionable modern options for literature adds so much depth to our kids' understanding of God's role in our human story.

In nearly every subject, we can incorporate biblical truths or at least recognize God's hand in all of creation. Even more, homeschooling allows us to parent very practically the way God commanded in Deuteronomy 6:6–7: "These commandments that I give you . . . are to be on your hearts. Impress them on your children.

Talk about them when you sit at home and when you walk along the road, when you lie down and when you get up." Recognizing how naturally we can do this has grown my love for homeschooling.

## 13. Homeschoolers Don't Have to Do Homework

When kids know what assignments need to be done each day, they can get them done on their own timeline. Unless my boys had an obligation during the day, they rarely needed to do schoolwork in the evening. Yet when they did have activities during the day (such as surfing, spearfishing, golfing, or competing in a debate tournament), they could choose to do their schoolwork early in the morning, in the evening, or on a weekend.

## 14. Homeschooling Supports Kids' Mental Health

Our youth today are experiencing an epidemic of anxiety and depression, and we know much of it is related to social pressures, academic stress, lack of sleep, and way too much screen time. (Of course the COVID-19 pandemic did not help either.)

Homeschool parents spend a lot of time with their kids, so we notice if something seems "off." We can talk to our kids or explore the root causes of mood or behavioral issues. We can get our kids the help they need and carve out time to work through difficult times without causing a great interruption in their schedule.

Even more, homeschoolers are spared most, if not all, of the negative peer interaction that contributes to mental health issues in a traditional school. Homeschooled kids are free to live and learn in a secure environment and grow up at their own pace. They also

> Homeschooled kids are free to live and learn in a secure environment and grow up at their own pace.

experience less pressure to be consumed by social media, which is a major factor in increased teenage mental health issues.[6]

## 15. Homeschooled Kids Can Get More Sleep and Can Adjust Their Schedule to Their Needs

Sleep is so important for our physical and mental health, and most kids (especially teens) don't get enough of it. One study published in *Behavioral Sleep Medicine* showed that homeschooled students slept on average ninety minutes more each night than kids attending traditional schools. (Interestingly, by the time the average homeschooler woke up, public and private school kids had been in class for eighteen minutes!)

Lisa Meltzer, a PhD and sleep psychologist, explained that melatonin (the hormone that helps regulate sleep) actually shifts during puberty, and often teens' sleep is deepest in the early morning hours. Because of this, even if a teenager wants to go to bed earlier, they often cannot fall asleep. Meltzer said that adolescents need nine hours of sleep a night, and those who attend school "are being asked to wake up and go to school at a time when their brains should physiologically be asleep."[7]

While it is good to work on a reasonable nighttime and morning schedule regardless of where your kids go to school (we are a work in progress on that front!), it is such a blessing to know that my homeschooled kids *can sleep in* if they need to. (And so can their mom, but that's another point I suppose. *wink*)

## 16. Homeschooled Kids Have Ample Time to Play, Use Their Imaginations, and Experience True Adventures

We will talk more about this in the chapters covering preschool and elementary school, but there is no doubt that homeschooling allows kids to be kids. My friend (and fellow homeschool mom) Jessica Smartt wrote one of my favorite parenting books called *Let Them Be Kids*. This excerpt from that book makes me want to jump and shout in agreement:

> Your kids need to see the Good Life. They need to have lived it, breathed it, and tasted it. They need to climb the mountains, see the views, experience the sweaty foreheads and skinned-up knees from a bona fide, heart-racing adventure. The world throws so much crap at them. Imitation fun. Phony entertainment. Fake joy. The world not only throws it at them, but kids are eating it up hook, line, and sinker. Depression and anxiety are at sky-high, unprecedented levels. While kids have access to higher levels of entertainment than any prior generation, they are far more bored and dissatisfied. They are the most technologically connected generation ever, but they report more loneliness.[8]

Indeed, homeschooling gives us the chance to give our kids the good life. I've seen it with my own eyes, and I wish it for every child growing up today!

## 17. Homeschooled Kids Have More Time to Spend with Grandparents or Other Special People in Their Lives

With the busyness of traditional school, activities, and homework, many kids have very little margin left to enjoy the most important people in their lives. Homeschooling changes that. As I write this, my youngest son is on the porch, helping his grandfather put together a shower chair for Levi's cousin who has muscular dystrophy and will be visiting us. Grandpa has done many projects at our house that Levi would have missed if he were away at school. What a blessing for my son to be able to spend time with his grandpa, learning how to put a piece of equipment together and doing something to serve his cousin—all during the forty-five minutes between math and history.

In the midst of a flexible school day, my boys have delivered a meal to a family from church, taken a coffee break with out-of-town guests, or picked up grandparents from the airport. And all that was possible simply because they were around during the day.

## 18. Homeschooled Kids Are Free to Be Themselves without the Pressure to Conform

Kids go through a lot of stages. They spend much of their growing-up time just trying to figure out who they are. What their interests are. How they want to dress. Who they admire or hope to be like. If the bulk of their time is spent in a traditional school setting, our children cannot help but be shaped by their peers. They are encouraged to like what everyone else likes. They feel pressure to conform, following the trends in clothing, music, and language.

Homeschooling gives kids a safe place just to be themselves. They can explore subjects based on what sincerely interests them, rather than based on popular opinion. They are set free from the petty pressures, the comparisons, and the fear of missing out that can lead to making bad decisions. I recall entire homeschool days with boys attired in pj's or a Spider-Man costume or a shirt and clip-on tie. (I tried not to ask questions.) Luke

> The homeschool environment offers our kids a secure foundation from which they can be delightfully themselves.

often created a fort for his cat to homeschool right next to him. Homeschooled kids can play Legos and dress up long after their peers have stopped doing these things (and pity the peers who wish they could too). The homeschool environment offers our kids a secure foundation from which they can be delightfully themselves. And that is one of my very favorite things.

## 19. Homeschooled Kids Are Physically Healthier

Research has shown that homeschooled children are thinner and leaner and have healthier diets than traditionally schooled children.[9] Being at home gives us an opportunity to feed our kids nourishing, home-cooked meals (and to teach them to eventually make their own). They are also not subject to the cafeteria food and exposed to all the junk that other kids might bring to school or purchase every day. Being at home also allows kids to exercise as they and their parents see fit. They are not stuck in a traditional classroom for hours on end every day. Instead, they can take frequent breaks and move around—or even do school standing up if they choose. It is easy to see, then, why homeschooled kids are not only fitter and leaner but also (as I've learned from experience) more likely to take these healthy habits with them into their future lives.

## 20. Homeschooled Students Grow Up to Be Amazing Adults

Homeschoolers usually grow up to be well-adjusted, balanced, and successful adults. Not only is this my opinion, but research backs it up. Studies have shown that adults who were homeschooled as kids are more likely than those who went to traditional school to

- volunteer or be involved in community service,
- be involved citizens, including voting in political elections,
- have good communication and social skills,[10]
- have lower rates of anxiety and mental health issues, and
- want to raise strong families of their own.[11]

Hello! That's some important data!

The handful of adults I know who were homeschooled are, indeed, really interesting, well-rounded, passionate people. One of them builds beautiful homes for a living; another writes books. One has raised millions of dollars to open and run a safehouse for sex-trafficked teenagers from all over the world. And another is homeschooling her own four kids. I have great respect for every one of them.

## My Favorite Part of Homeschooling?

Recently in yet another attempt to declutter my storage closet, I pulled out a few bins of memorabilia from my older sons' elementary years. Nostalgia flooded me as I sorted through little-boy spelling tests, a rolled-up poster from a sixth-grade Hubble telescope science project, and a ziplock bag full of shells collected after a big winter swell. In that quiet moment, I closed my eyes and could nearly hear the laughter of little boys, feel the warm school-morning snuggles, and smell the ocean in the shells in front of me.

Just then a ringing phone startled me out of my memories, and I picked up to hear my college-age son Jonah on the other end of the line. "Hey, Mom, just had to tell you—I aced my physics exam!"

My favorite part of homeschooling? I'll never be able to answer that.

And I have a feeling you won't either.

### TAKE-HOME THOUGHT
---

There are a lot of great reasons to homeschool your kids; some of the biggest will be easily treasured in your heart, though they may be hard to put on paper.

## REFLECTION QUESTION

———

Which of the twenty reasons to homeschool
resonated with you most?

## CHAPTER 2

# THE LIFE THEY'LL THANK YOU FOR LATER (PART 2)

## 10 Things Homeschoolers Get to Avoid

It's easy to talk about everything I love about homeschooling. I had to cut myself off sharing my top twenty list with you in the previous chapter. But another great reason to homeschool has to do with all that homeschooling is *not*—in other words, all that homeschooling allows kids *to avoid*.

A 2023 Washington Post-Schar School poll reported that "home-schoolers today are likely to be motivated by fear of school shootings, anxiety over bullying and anger with the perceived encroachment of politics into public schools."[1] This, of course, is just part of the list, so next, let's touch on some of those things homeschooled *kids get to avoid*.

## 1. Homeschoolers Avoid School Violence

As mentioned above, a lot of parents today will say that a fear of school shootings is a top motivator for their decision to homeschool.

And for good reason. Up until 2017, the United States saw about eleven school shootings a year. In 2018 school violence climbed, and then except for a brief pause during the pandemic (when schools were shut down), school shootings climbed to forty-two in 2021 and then to forty-six in 2022.[2]

I've spoken with friends who are trying to reassure their anxious public school children while also battling their own anxiety about sending their child to school every day. There has been a massive increase in the sales of children's bulletproof backpacks,[3] and active shooter drills are a normal and required part of school. Even if a child never experiences a school shooting (which we can assume most will not), all of these "safety measures" can be trauma inducing on their own. Yet this is the reality school-going kids live with.

The good news is: Homeschooled kids don't face the risk of school shootings or the fear and anxiety related to all they see on the news about that topic. While none of us is promised another day (only God is sovereign, and he numbers our days), I think we can all agree that we would prefer our kids be educated in an environment where they aren't always fearful for their own safety or preparing for the worst.

## 2. Homeschoolers Avoid Negative Socialization

Socialization is one of the first reasons parents give for *not* wanting to homeschool their kids—and we'll talk more about that in chapter 3. But I cannot resist briefly flipping the script on that topic to share my heartfelt opinion: avoiding the kind of socialization that goes on in public (and many private) schools is one of my greatest reasons for homeschooling!

From bad attitudes to bad words, from peer pressure to porn on phones, I am happy to say a big "No thank you" to the kind of socialization that goes on in a typical modern school setting. We can all agree that kids need to learn social skills. But my own kids—as well as countless others—are proof that this can be done—and done well—in a homeschool environment. In fact, the comment I get most from people who encounter my older sons (or interview Luke about his surfing) is, "Wow! Your boys are so comfortable talking to adults!" Then they go on to tell me how impressed they are with their conversation skills, their ability to make eye contact, the thoughtfulness they show to people around them, and on and on.

It is important to note that all the qualities I just listed—the things most people consider "good social skills"—were taught to our boys by their parents. They did not learn them from their peers. Because we had time with them, all day, every day, my husband and I had the opportunity to teach and train and model proper ways to interact with the world around them. When people comment on our kids' social skills, we've half-jokingly called it "the homeschool effect."

I don't say this to brag but because it's true—and because I would honestly love to do away with the socialization myth. (It does get old.) Frankly, I have much greater concern about the socialization that goes on in a traditional school setting than the perceived lack of socialization in a homeschool setting.

## 3. Homeschoolers Avoid Unnecessary Exposure to Drugs and Alcohol

We all know the devastation that drugs and alcohol have done in our society. Depending on the region you live in, you probably hear sickening statistics about opioids, meth, or fentanyl destroying young lives.

Yet these heavier drugs usually begin with something less shocking. Marijuana is a gateway drug that leads to harder drugs.

Teenagers often consider underage drinking a rite of passage. Then, year after year, drunk driving accidents are one of the highest causes of death among teenagers. Nicotine is also highly addictive (and ultimately deadly in the form of cancer), and the current vaping methods pack higher levels of nicotine than traditional cigarettes.

Most teens haven't yet developed the mental maturity to reason through the risks associated with substance use, and studies show that peer pressure is the number one reason adolescents begin experimenting with illegal substances.[4]

A slow comfortability comes with prolonged exposure to things. Perhaps at first kids are shocked when they see or hear about friends at school who are drinking underage or smoking pot regularly, but the sheer number of times they are exposed to it will tend to normalize the behavior.

We know that homeschooled kids may also be exposed to substances, especially if they are involved in sports or other activities. Our kids were not shielded from exposure to drugs and alcohol in the surf and skate community they were raised in. But I am convinced that the conversations we had at home, combined with the positive environment in which our boys spent most of their days, gave them an aversion to all these things, rather than an interest or curiosity in them. And this is true for most homeschoolers. Research shows that homeschooled adolescents are less likely to smoke, vape, or use drugs or alcohol, and are more likely to avoid having friends who might influence them to experiment with these things.[5]

## 4. Homeschoolers Avoid (Most) Bullying

There may be nothing more gut-wrenching for a parent than sending a child off to school, knowing they may—or will—be the target of bullies. The National Bullying Prevention Center reported that more than 49 percent of tweens (nine to twelve years old) said they experienced bullying at school. And sadly, being bullied is highly associated with anxiety, depression, and suicide. Studies show that the most common places bullying occur are in the hallway or stairwell at *school* (43 percent), inside the (*school*) classroom (42 percent), in the (*school*) cafeteria (27 percent), outside on *school* grounds (22 percent), online or by text (15 percent), in the (*school*) bathroom or locker room (12 percent), and on the *school* bus (8 percent).[6] I don't think I need to point out the common (*school*) denominator.

I have heard heartbreaking stories of kids who endured years of bullying, and even after they left the school environment where it happened, they carried the trauma with them into adulthood. One of my friends whose brother had this experience said, "I can't emphasize enough the damage that a bully (who, let's be honest, is just a kid who doesn't really know any better) can do to a child. If that is happening to your child, *move your kid to a new environment ASAP*, whether to a new school or homeschool. It's not worth it to stay another day."

Homeschooling provides kids with a safe and secure environment to get through the challenging tween and teenage years. There will still be difficulties, and they might even face bullies in other places (in the neighborhood, in sports, or—like one of my own sons' experience that I share in my book *Boy Mom*—sometimes at a church youth group), but these experiences won't compare to the damage done through daily exposure to bullies in a school setting.

## 5. Homeschoolers Avoid the Teaching of Evolutionism as Fact

Since formal, school-sponsored Bible readings and prayer were ruled out of public school classrooms in 1960, the anti-God momentum has only grown. The theory of evolution is widely accepted in public schools as the *only* reasonable and "factual" explanation for the existence of humankind, not to mention all life on earth, to the exclusion of God. And only a few states allow the alternative of an intelligent design, creation-based explanation to be presented alongside evolution.[7]

As homeschool parents, we get to choose the subject matter our kids are exposed to. Even more importantly, we can teach our kids to think critically, allowing them time to ask questions, study various viewpoints, understand biases, and consider both biblical and scientific facts—which, I am so glad to know, are not in conflict.

## 6. Homeschoolers Avoid Gender Indoctrination

Parents are the very best people to teach their kids God's design for sexuality and gender. No matter where parents stand on issues of gender and sexuality, I think we can agree that trusting a government institution to educate our kids on such a vital and fragile topic is dangerous.

A school administration's stance on gender issues will impact what is being allowed, encouraged, and promoted in the classroom. Research done by *City Journal*, a publication of the Manhattan Institute for Policy Research, looked at a large group of eighteen- to twenty-year-olds and found that more than 90 percent of the students reported some form of public school exposure to both critical race theory and critical gender concepts.[8] (We'll touch on race in a moment.)

Many public schools today proudly assert that they are offering a "safe place" for kids to explore their sexuality and gender, leaving parents out of these critically important conversations. School districts across America are allowing students to change their names, pronouns, or gender expression—without parental consent and often without notification.

Parents interviewed for a *New York Times* article expressed the frustration of discovering their child's "preferred name" scribbled on a piece of paper at the bottom of their backpack or finding out that the school knew more about their child's gender confusion than they did.[9]

Books featuring same-sex partners or queer or transgender characters are being read aloud in early elementary classrooms. And that's only skimming the surface of policies taught or endorsed by the school faculty, or cultural trends encouraged by adults who don't share your perspective on raising children.

In contrast, homeschooling families have the opportunity to introduce their kids to the topics of sexuality and gender as they are ready. Parents can also prepare kids for the cultural issues they will face outside of their home. I am incredibly grateful to have spared my sons the complicated and messy social situations that kids simply are not developmentally ready to handle at a young age. By the time my sons went away to college, they had a firm grip on the truth about their sexuality and identity from God's Word. They were also prepared with kind and gracious responses (still grounded in the truth) to situations they would face while away from home.

For this and the next point, I think it is wise to follow the words of Colossians 2:8: "See to it that no one takes you captive by philosophy and empty deceit, according to human tradition, according to the elemental spirits of the world, and not according to Christ" (ESV).

## 7. Homeschoolers Avoid Learning about Racial Issues from a Biased Viewpoint

We can all agree that our world needs racial healing and unity more than ever. The past few years have taught us that we have far to go and much to learn on this topic. Yet trusting schools to shape our children's perspective on racial issues is dangerous. Our children are vulnerable to the biased viewpoints and opinions they hear from adults (which could lean in any direction), especially when there is not also an emphasis on helping kids develop critical thinking skills.

Parents have the responsibility of teaching kids that God created all people, in a beautiful variety of shades, as part of *the human race*. It is our job to introduce our kids to many cultures and the rich history behind them. We should also help our kids understand what racism is and what we can do (especially as people of faith) to work toward racial unity and healing.

Tony Evans offers much wisdom on this topic. In an article in the *Dallas Morning News*, he wrote, "This individual transformation then must flow into the family as parents transfer these values to their children. We cannot expect people to think differently and act differently if they aren't hearing differently from their parents, if they are not getting a righteous value system of judging people by the content of their character, not the color of their skin."[10]

Evans consistently points to the responsibility of *the parents and the church*—not the schools—for teaching our children about racial issues. And for good reason: it is our responsibility. The home is where values like these are best taught.

## 8. Homeschoolers Avoid Pressure to Date before They Are Ready

I remember my first experience of true dating peer pressure—in third grade! As crazy as that now sounds, I distinctly recall my peer group coaching me on exactly how to place my hand next to my crush's leg during a class movie so he might get the hint to hold my hand. Though I was mostly a tomboy up to that point (raised with only brothers!), from that time on, it seemed like all my friends and

I talked about was boys. Looking back, I see how the environment of my public school days normalized dating way before I was ready and opened the door to some bad decisions as I grew up.

In contrast, my sons did not date at all during their home-schooling years. I am pretty sure this was due to a combination of things: They grew up in an all-boy household, and they were home-schooled—in the country. We didn't have stated rules about dating, but we had plenty of good conversations about their futures and God's plans for them. Dating in high school didn't really fit any of that. They kept busy doing sports and other healthy things. They weren't in a hurry.

Our boys developed a great group of friends through youth group and sports, but everyone remained at friend status. Looking back, they now confess they had crushes growing up, and they looked forward to dating eventually, but they were learning to be young men of character who were patient and focused on other things. Between having excellent role models in their youth lead-ers and spending several years reading from the book of Proverbs daily, they were guided by wisdom rather than by the culture.

Regardless of a family's position on dating, homeschooled students get to avoid the unnecessary pressure to date that often comes with a traditional school environment. And because of the time spent together, parents have the opportunity to guide and coach their kids as they navigate all of these things.

## 9. Homeschoolers Avoid the Comparison Trap

I love some healthy competition and encourage my boys to con-sider the rat race of life awaiting them out there "in the big world." But an element of unnecessary pressure comes with a daily school environment where kids feel ranked by grades or standardized test scores and are constantly comparing current accomplishments and future goals. Comparison goes beyond grades and test scores, of course, as kids also rank one another based on appearance and popularity, social media following, sports achievements, financial status, and more.

I remember a particular visit from friends whose kids were a couple years older than my boys and were about to graduate from public high school on the mainland. The older kids were comparing their SAT scores and joking about which one had closer to a perfect score. At this point, Josiah had just taken his PSAT test (practicing for the SAT later), and I could see his face fall at the older kids' bragging. Suddenly this test that, to him, represented all kinds of excitement and potential was turning into a heavy weight of comparison.

Yes, comparison will always be a part of life. As they grew up, my boys all became aware of social rankings. And eventually they would discover that certain test scores were necessary to get into certain colleges and they would face the pressure to get a competitive score. But I am so grateful that because they were homeschooled, test score comparisons and social pressures were not constantly in their faces. Homeschooling provided my sons with a secure environment, free from the pressures that can deflate kids before they've even had a chance to begin something.

## 10. Homeschoolers Avoid Feeling Stuck

When I ran this chapter concept by Luke and asked for his input, one of the first things he said was: "I am so glad I wasn't forced to go through the daily grind of a monotonous school schedule and years of feeling stuck in an institutional environment." Ah, yes. Luke has enjoyed the freedom of his homeschool life.

I have heard stories of the frustration that many schoolkids feel as a result of having very few options. They go to the school they are "zoned for" and get the teachers they are assigned. They are required to sit in desks and behave, and they're likely to be sent to the principal (or an ADHD specialist) if they are wiggly or talkative or do not conform. Kids who learn differently or need to move a little extra or have thoughts that don't sound like everyone else's can have a very hard time in a traditional school setting.

Contrast that with a homeschool setting in which families can choose a curriculum that fits their child's learning style and provide their kids with an environment where they have the freedom to move around physically, converse about what they're learning, and develop critical thinking skills. Students flourish when they are heard, loved, and supported. This doesn't mean we coddle our kids or never make them do things they don't enjoy. (Just ask my boys.) It simply means that our kids don't feel stuck. Institutionalized. They have options. We can change things up, try new things, and find what works best. We might tweak their diet or their sleep schedule or add some exercise to their mornings (which I highly recommend). But they have freedom and choices. And isn't that how we hope they will approach the rest of life!?

## What Else?

We could go on and on with more things that homeschooled kids get to avoid—from homework to cafeteria food to chasing after the school bus every morning because you're running late (oh wait, maybe that was just my childhood). My list of "things to avoid" may align with some of your concerns about traditional schools, or you may have other concerns to add to the list. But let's keep one thing in mind: homeschooling is so much more than an alternative to other forms of school. Even if my boys had the chance to go to the very best school with the very best faculty and curriculum— and our personal choice of peers—I would still choose our simple homeschool life all over again. (Most days, anyway!)

The bottom line is that by being homeschooled, kids get to be informed about issues related to sexuality, gender, race, politics, and whatever might be next in our cultural conversation through the filter of loving parents who want the best for their kids *and for the world they will grow up in.* As I suggest in *Raising Amazing*, "It's not only part of our job but a high calling on our part to be a guiding influence, and to 'set the first tracks' for our kids."[11] We do this by talking with them about these crucial issues *before* they learn about them elsewhere. And no doubt the most effective way to do this is in the safety of our own homes.

## TAKE-HOME THOUGHT

Homeschoolers get to avoid regular exposure to most of
the things that are tearing apart our culture today.

## REFLECTION QUESTION

Which of the ten things that homeschooled kids
get to avoid most resonates with you?

CHAPTER 3

# WHY NOT?

## 11 Reasons Families Don't Try Homeschooling (or Don't Stick with It)

Perhaps some people grow up dreaming of homeschooling their children one day. But I'm pretty sure they are not the majority. Most homeschool parents I know are more like me. They've taken a lot of time and thought and have spent sleepless nights wrestling with God (just kidding—sort of) in their process of deciding to become homeschoolers. Along the way, most of us asked questions and came up with some good excuses (or so we thought) why we could "never homeschool" our kids. (Add dramatic voice to that statement.)

*Tell me you've said it too?*

Perhaps in braver moments, we've looked those excuses straight in the eye and asked ourselves if they are indeed truly good or if they're actually just smoke screens—excuses for not doing something we know deep down we could *and should* do. Or maybe some of our "excuses" were legit but not necessarily deal-breakers. Perhaps, with a few adjustments or compromises, we realized we *could* homeschool our kids. And many of us who did end up deciding to homeschool are so glad we chose to find a way to make it happen.

Through conversations with homeschoolers and non-homeschoolers alike, I have found that there are some common reasons for thinking, *I could never homeschool my kids.* Some of these are very good reasons—downright legit and worthy of serious consideration.

Other "reasons," though? Well, I might just have to call your bluff (as only a true friend would).

So now, being as fair and balanced as I can, with all the big-sister love in my heart, I will respond to the top reasons I have encountered for why parents don't think they can homeschool their kids.

> Note: Because homeschooling (like life) is not perfect and there are some very real challenges even in the most ideal homeschool setting, I wrote a bonus chapter to address some of the most common challenges to homeschooling—and some helpful/creative solutions for each challenge. You can find the link to this bonus chapter titled: "Practical Help for Real Homeschool Challenges" in the resource section.

## Reason #1: "I Don't Want My Kids to Miss Out on Socialization" (aka "I'm Afraid Homeschooling Would Make My Kids Weird")

*Ah, I've been looking forward to responding to this one! I already touched on the socialization topic in the last chapter, but it's worth touching on again.*

When you bring up the "socialization" question to a seasoned homeschool mom, you might want to prepare for a few different responses. On a good day, we'll be kind and understanding. (Remember, most of us used to think the same thing.) But after hearing it so many (many, many) times, we tend to get weary, so then you might experience our snarky side. (Please forgive us.)

Your socialization concern might be because you had a great school experience yourself; perhaps you made lifelong friends and cannot imagine not giving your child the same experience. You might have an introverted child and fear that if they do school at home, they'll never develop any social skills. Maybe you've met some homeschooled kids who really *are* weird. (I have too.) In response to these concerns, let me offer a few thoughts.

First, if you had a great school experience—one that you'd love for your child to replicate—it is important to acknowledge that our world has changed. Whatever school and friends and a "social life" looked like back when you were growing up is not what they look like now. Even if you're a young parent. And there are a few reasons why.

We could spend the rest of this book talking about the effects that technology—specifically social media—is having on our youth today. But suffice it to say that socially, it changes *everything*. I suppose it will be decades before we discover the ramifications of teenagers who spend an average of 4.8 hours a day on social media.[1] (And I think that is a conservative number.) But if we hope to even begin to swim upstream on this one, "socializing" kids in a public school will not be in your best interest. The current is strong there, and the odds are not in your favor.

Further, if your child is a Christian and not afraid to say so, they are likely to face social challenges at school that you and I did not. Today's culture puts a great focus on tolerance for all kinds of lifestyles—often except those from a "narrow" biblical viewpoint. In fact, tolerance alone is no longer enough; our culture wants affirmation and endorsement. These things make it incredibly challenging for Bible-believing students to enjoy a positive, supportive environment in most traditional school settings. Instead, they are likely to be targeted as bigoted and closed-minded, even if their only crime is standing strong for their belief system and doing their best to love others without approving of sinful behaviors. (Note: Some Christian kids will be ready to handle this, yes. But it's too big a burden for most kids to carry. See more under #9 "I Want My Kids to be 'Lights' in Their School," later in this chapter.)

Second, the idea of "socializing" children by placing them in an environment with a massive group of same-age peers is simply not true or good socialization. There is no other time in life when they will live or work in such a setting. Children are best socialized by doing life in an environment where they interact with a variety of people from many age groups. And they don't need to be with a lot of people all day every day. In fact, many kids get overwhelmed and overstimulated when they are constantly around a lot of people. It's not necessary nor preparatory for anything they will face in their future.

> Children are best socialized by doing life in an environment where they interact with a variety of people from many age groups.

Don't imagine for a moment that homeschooling your child means they never mix it up with friends but will hole up in their bedroom until they turn forty. Not even close. Most homeschooled kids I know have a healthy social life—participating in co-ops, doing sports, and participating in many other activities, which we'll talk about in future chapters. The difference is, *you get to choose* those activities and who your kids do them with.

My boys have grown up in the country, spending most of their days with their siblings and parents, a dog and a cat, and a lot of fresh air. After school, they've participated in sports and gone to youth group, and in between everything, they've spent a lot of time with all kinds of people. And, as I said previously, I cannot count how many people have gone out of their way to tell me how impressed they are with my sons' social skills.

Third, about the "weird kid" concern—I like to respond to that one with a question of my own: For all the weird homeschooled kids you've met (because indeed, they are out there), can you think of any strange kids you or your kids have gone to public school with? I sure can. I can recall at least two handfuls of really odd kids from the public schools I grew up in. And no one thought two seconds about it. There are weird kids and strange people everywhere!

Here's what I typically tell people who get stuck on this weird-kid issue: Kids typically grow up to be a lot like their parents, especially if they spend a lot of time with them. So if you're a little bit on the odd side and you homeschool your kids, then sure, your kids are likely to grow up to be a bit odd. But if you think of yourself as pretty cool and mostly normal, you can anticipate your kids growing up to be pretty cool and mostly normal too.

I can think of a few homeschooled kids who fit the stereotypical nerd persona. And when I met their parents, it made sense. And you know what? These kids grew up to be successful, funny, and great contributors to society. There are much worse things than raising kids who are on the nerd spectrum (see chapter 2 for the list). When you think about it, some of the most successful people in the eyes of the world fit in this category. (Elon Musk and Mark Zuckerberg come to mind. Even if we don't point to them as role models, they are, without a doubt, smart, financially successful, and *pretty nerdy too*.)

## Reason #2: "I Don't Have the Patience" (Commonly Said Along With "My Child and I Will Butt Heads")

Wow, can I ever relate! Funny thing is, I thought I was a patient person—until I had kids! (Anyone else?) No doubt, parenting tests our character and highlights any lack of patience that might have been lurking below the surface. If your kids already test your patience, then the thought of homeschooling might sound completely unreasonable to you. Sending your kids to school might seem like the very break you need to stay sane so you can be patient when your kids are at home.

I could say much more on this "patience" topic, but I'll be fairly brief here. First, you must trust that I'm not lying to you when I say this: many homeschool parents (myself included) find themselves with *more patience* when we begin homeschooling than we had before. Truly. I used to lose my patience almost daily during the early morning rush to get my kids off to preschool. Then I would spend the remainder of the day haunted by the fact that I'd dropped them off at school with a negative start to their day. I still shudder when I remember a few bad mornings, one in particular when we were rushing out the door—late again for preschool—and I couldn't find Jonah, who was maybe four years old at the time. When I discovered him upstairs in the bathroom, happily seated on the potty going number two . . . I lost my last nerve. Screaming at my young son all the way to school that morning for the unthinkable crime of stopping to poop when we were already late for school was a parenting low. Times like these gave me good reason to question whether I had the patience to homeschool my kids.

> Many homeschool parents find themselves with *more patience* when we begin homeschooling than we had before.

But here's what I discovered: once we started homeschooling, our days were no longer constantly rushed. There was no (daily) outside pressure to be anywhere or do anything. Because I thrive in a semi-structured environment, I still woke everyone up at a regular time and tried to keep a schedule, but we also had much more freedom in our days. If we'd had a hard night or something came up in the morning (like a child's need to poop!), it wasn't the end of the world. We could simply adjust, reset, and move on.

Homeschooling offers plenty of moments when your kids will push your buttons and you will struggle mightily with patience, but from my experience (and from the experience of many others I have spoken to), homeschooling relieves so much pressure from your life and your kids' lives that patience isn't the big deal most of us at one time imagined it would be.

Second—and this is said with some tough love—if you lack the patience to homeschool, that may be the very reason you should do it. I mean, if you lacked strength in your biceps, I'd suggest you start doing bicep curls regularly. In time you'll gain strength in those biceps, right? In the same way, you will grow in patience as you work that "muscle."

Patience is a defining aspect of love (see 1 Corinthians 13:4), and it also made Paul's list of "fruits of the Spirit" in Galatians 5. Every person pursuing spiritual maturity ought to pray for and strive to develop patience. Homeschooling your kids may be just the tool God uses to help with this.

Practically speaking, one approach I have taken in developing my own patience is to play a little game where I imagine there is a hidden camera (or even better—Jesus himself) somewhere in my living room as I face some of the most patience-trying moments. When I reviewed multiplication tables for the ninety-ninth time or helped kids sound out the simplest vowel sounds (smiling and breathing deeply through gritted teeth), it helped if I viewed these things as a little test of my character. Each time I got through a challenging lesson or lovingly yet firmly disciplined a child with a bad attitude, I smiled to my imaginary hidden camera (and to the Lord), recognizing another small victory.

Instead of avoiding the opportunity to develop more patience,

I encourage you to see homeschooling as a great way to be a grown-up and practice (yes, *practice*) patience. Don't run from it—embrace it.

## Reason #3: "I Don't Have the Education Necessary to Homeschool My Kids"

I respect a parent's concern about their own education being a factor in homeschooling their children. However, if this is one of your major obstacles, I have good news for you! Research shows that your kids will be better off academically if you homeschool them than if you send them to public school. Homeschooled students score above average on achievement tests *regardless of their parents' level of formal education.*[2]

It is also good to note that by high school, homeschooled kids typically spend the majority of their day doing schoolwork independently. You don't have to prepare yourself to teach ancient history or statistics. (My sons surpassed my ability to help them in math and science education by the time they were in ninth grade—and I have a bachelor of science in sports medicine.) They also went on to take AP courses and pass advanced placement exams—*without a formal, on-site teacher.* Plenty of resources are available to teach what we cannot.

In fact, my sons have told me that they felt very prepared for the challenging courses they faced in college because they had quite literally "learned how to learn" during high school. When they hit difficult points in their studies, they went back and reread a chapter or rewatched a video, sometimes multiple times—which, by the way, is how we will learn things for the rest of our lives!

As Dorothy Sayers said, "For the sole true end of education is simply this: to teach men how to learn for themselves; and whatever instruction fails to do this is effort spent in vain."[3]

# Reason #4: "I Have to Work"

Whether you are a single parent or are in a situation where both parents need to work to support the family, you may assume you cannot homeschool your kids. This may very well be a valid obstacle to homeschooling, but I'll offer a few things to consider before dismissing the possibility.

Once again, I have good news: most of the time it is possible to work and homeschool!

One benefit of homeschooling is that you are not on someone else's timeline. You can make a school schedule work around your job or lifestyle. Some families do year-round school (with breaks, of course) and therefore have shorter official school days. Your kids might do some or all of their schoolwork in the mornings or evenings. You might recruit extended family to help with homeschooling, swap days with another working/homeschooling parent, or hire a helper. (I have hired homeschooled high school girls to help with my younger kids a few days a week in various busy seasons of book writing and homeschooling.) There are websites dedicated to working homeschool parents, and finding a like-minded community to connect with may give you the confidence you need. (See the resource section for links.) Over at the Working Homeschool Mom Club website, Jen Mackinnon says, "I believe **every working mom** can homeschool their children while enjoying life. You just need a little help with the **right tools and systems** in your toolbox, a little inspiration, a little encouragement, and a **BIG dose of community** to keep going when things get tough."[4]

I feel like I must address the "have to" part of this obstacle, specifically for the two-parent households reading this. While there are situations in which both parents need to work to put food on the table and keep the lights on, often both parents work more to keep up a lifestyle than out of necessity. I know of families who have downsized, sold a car, given up a summer vacation, become serious about a budget, or simplified in several ways to allow one parent to stay home as much as necessary to educate their children. When we want something badly enough, we can get creative about attaining it, and there really are a lot of options. (There are also excellent resources and support options for single parents who homeschool. See the resource section for more on that.)

My son Luke has said that what we have given him through the time commitment of homeschooling has been more valuable than any material things we could have given him. In his opinion (and his brothers all agree), homeschooling is the most worthwhile investment a parent can make in the lives of their kids.

You might consider if some version of your work (or a different job altogether) could be done from home. I have full confidence that there are options available for most parents who want to continue to make a living while homeschooling their kids. (I'm typing this on a laptop while my son does a math worksheet next to me.) I have been a full-time homeschool mom juggling a writing and speaking career on the side for twelve years, and while I have very little "spare time" (ahem, social life), I wouldn't trade either of my "jobs" for anything.

## Reason #5: "I Don't Have the Support of My Spouse"

This one is tough. And not unusual (especially initially). As I shared earlier, my husband was not excited about the idea of homeschooling when I first mentioned the possibility, and I remember the stress that caused.

One parent is often skeptical of—or even strongly opposed to—the idea of homeschooling. If this is your situation, before throwing in the towel too quickly, take some time to ask God for wisdom. Consider the most effective way to approach the conversation with your spouse. Maybe they would be open to reading this book (or parts of it). If the conversation becomes too stressful or heated, you might consider bringing a trusted friend or counselor in to help you communicate your thoughts. You could also suggest a "trial run" of homeschooling, where you decide to homeschool for a year to see how it goes. If you do it well, your spouse is likely to end the year with a completely different mindset.

## Reason #6: "I Am Divorced and Share the Custody of My Kids"

If you share custody with another parent, homeschooling can certainly be challenging. I recently spent time with a young lady who was homeschooled in her elementary years until her parents divorced before she started middle school. She said her mom tried to keep homeschooling her and her sisters, but on the weeks they went to their dad's house it was complicated and chaotic. She said that it was not only hard to keep up on school, but the situation also seemed to cause more conflict between her parents. She described the relief it was when they all finally started going to a public school. School became one of the things in life that felt consistent and stable. Years later when she became a Christian, she could see God's hand on her through that difficult season. Her story broke my heart, but I could appreciate the positive role her school played in that difficult season.

I have heard of parents who successfully homeschool after a divorce, but I understand that is likely the exception, not the norm. I would applaud any parents who share custody who are able to work out a homeschool lifestyle that works for the children. I think with some creativity and a commitment to the kids' best, this *can be done*. However, I understand that it might be very difficult.

If you wish you could homeschool but cannot because of a

custody arrangement, I would encourage you to commit to being involved in your kids' school to whatever extent that you can. Pray for them and with them. Your role in their life and the attitude, faith, and character you model as you walk through this challenging season will likely impact your kids more than you will know for many years. God can fill in gaps and move mountains, and he will be ever present for your children.

## Reason #7: "My Child/Children Don't Want to Be Homeschooled"

Feeling called to homeschool but having kids who are not interested can be challenging. If this is your situation, I absolutely recommend having some good, honest conversations with your kids about how they feel. What is their reason for not wanting to be homeschooled? Do they have a preconceived idea about what it will be like? Do they love their social life at school? Listen to whatever is on their minds and don't argue with them. If they feel heard and cared about, they are more likely to be open to what you are suggesting.

Some kids are uncomfortable with change and don't want to try something new. Some kids are worried they won't see their friends anymore if they don't go to school. Kids might be aware of academic or extracurricular opportunities at a school that they would miss out on if they homeschooled. There are plenty of reasons kids may want to remain in a traditional school, and some of them may be worthy of consideration!

However, you know your child best, and you have the wisdom of a vantage point that kids simply don't have. If you believe that homeschooling is the best option for your child, then present it to them in a thoughtful and respectful way. Remember, you are the parent. You are responsible for making good choices on behalf of your child, whether they like those choices or not. In fact, in a Q&A episode on Heidi St. John's *Off the Bench* podcast, Heidi responded to this question by saying that it is unfair to "burden" our kids with the choice of how to do school. Children look to their parents to know what is best, and we are wise to lead them confidently in that. And though it may be difficult in the moment, there is an excellent chance they'll thank us for it later.

Jonah really wanted to try going to public school during his sophomore year of high school. He wanted to play sports on a high school team, and he was curious about the social aspect of attending public school. The more he talked about it, the more he started to convince me. *Maybe it would be better for him,* I began to reason.

When I looked into sending Jonah to school, I learned that our public school district does not allow homeschooled students to register past the ninth grade. That means that if a homeschooler wanted to start after ninth grade, no matter how smart or well-educated they were, they would have to go back and begin again as a ninth grader. (Interesting rule, right?) This idea did not sit well with Jonah, so he chose to continue to homeschool. Now that he is a college student, he is so glad for that "inconvenient" rule. In his words, "Most of the reason I wanted to go to school was to be with friends, but the friends I wanted to be with would not have been good for me anyway."

## Reason #8: "I Have Health Issues That Would Make It Difficult to Homeschool"

If your family is dealing with a chronic health issue, that could make it very difficult to homeschool. If only one parent is available to homeschool and that parent is going through serious medical treatments, is struggling with mental illness, or is dealing with some other extreme case, first, I am so sorry. I imagine it must be incredibly challenging for you to parent, let alone consider home-schooling, at this time in your life.

In this case, it is possible that a student might benefit from a learning environment away from home. As with other points on this list, there might be some creative options if you take the time to think outside the box. I know of grandparents who love the idea of helping with homeschooling, as well as young adults who have created a business of being homeschool tutors for busy families. There are many variables and there is grace for every season. But I do encourage you to prayerfully consider the options, get some counsel, and navigate life and parenting one season at a time. You can always revisit the idea of homeschooling in the future, even if the current timing is not good. And never forget that you can still be a great parent and teach your kids amazing things in the time you do spend with them!

## Reason #9: "I Want My Kids to Be 'Lights' in Their School"

Hang in there with me on this one, because I think it is a very important line of thought to address. The idea of our kids being "salt and light" in their schools comes from Jesus's famous Sermon on the Mount passage in Matthew 5:13–16. I love the idea of raising kids to be young evangelists, but there are many problems with using these verses as a reason to send our kids to school.

For starters, we can note that Jesus spoke these words to his (grown) disciples, not to a group of children. It takes time for children to come to a mature understanding of their faith in such a way that they are prepared to communicate and defend it well. It is not reasonable to burden our kids with the expectation that they might stand for truth (day after day) in an environment that is likely to be opposed to biblical truth.

Interestingly, a passage where Jesus *was* speaking specifically in reference to children is Matthew 19:14: "Let the little children *come to me*, and do not hinder them, for the kingdom of heaven belongs to such as these" (emphasis mine). So, while adults are called to *go out into the world to be salt and light,* Jesus simply told the children to "come." Leading our kids to the Lord is our number one job. Then, as they grow in maturity, they will eventually be ready to go out into the world to shine their light and make disciples.

Not only is it unreasonable to expect kids to evangelize their peers from a young age, but realistically, they are often the ones who will get "evangelized" by the belief system of their peers or teachers. When you're learning to walk on the "narrow path," you need a supportive environment.

In their early years, our children need to learn about Christ. Our job as parents is to "train up a child in the way he should go" (Proverbs 22:6 ESV). We are called to bring up our kids in the "training and instruction of the Lord" (Ephesians 6:4). In Deuteronomy 6:6–7, God gave Moses a clear picture of what it would look like to bring up kids this way: "And these words that I command you today shall be on your heart. You shall teach them diligently to your children, and shall talk of them when you sit in your house, and when you walk by the way, and when you lie down, and when you rise" (ESV).

> In their early years, our children need to learn about Christ. Our job as parents is to "train up a child in the way he should go" (Proverbs 22:6 ESV).

Our kids are vulnerable to peer pressure and are influenced by the environment they spend time in. Proverbs 13:20 says, "Whoever walks with the wise becomes wise, but the companion of fools will suffer harm" (ESV). Kids attending school all day will be surrounded by all kinds of kids, including plenty who would fall into the category of what King Solomon called "fools." Children do not all have the spiritual discernment and maturity needed to represent and defend their relationship with Christ in a spiritually hostile environment.

Growing in a mature understanding of the Bible and developing a biblical worldview takes time and intentionality. A homeschool environment makes it possible to focus on this consistently.

We have made God's Word a foundation of our boys' education, and as a family, we encourage one another to share the gospel in whatever environment we are in. Luke recalls talking to kids at the skate park about Jesus when he was eight or nine years old, and all our boys have a heart to communicate the gospel clearly. Josiah is especially passionate about sharing his faith—he is active in an international ministry, shares his faith regularly in the surf lineup (there are some good breaks between waves), and if you're lucky enough to sit by him on the airplane, you're likely to get to chat about Jesus. This all began by teaching our boys about God's love and truth as they grew up. But this is very different from sending kids to school, where they are likely to be one of very few Jesus followers in a crowd of nonbelievers.

Josiah recalls encountering a fellow Christian at his small Christian college. When they were discussing their respective childhoods, she claimed that after being homeschooled for a time, she had been sent to public high school to "shine her light." At first this sounded admirable, but strange to Josiah were her inappropriate language and worldly lifestyle. Josiah suggested that had his friend better prepared for the public school setting, she might have been more than prepared for college. Yet this wasn't the case. Josiah's conclusion was that this friend had gone through life backward: it may have been better for her to develop a more robust character at home and then attend college—secular or Christian—when she was mature enough to "shine her light."

## Reason #10: "I Send My Kids to School for Academics and Teach Them about God at Home and in Church"

Sending kids to school for academics and letting them learn about the Bible at home and in church has become a socially acceptable idea in the modern Christian community. Similar to the last point, it sounds pretty good at first. But I want to point out two important considerations in response to this idea. First, there is no such thing as a spiritually neutral education. And second, even if there were, that idea does not fit with God's call to us as parents.

There is no neutral education. It is impossible to receive an education devoid of spiritual bias. From the origin of humans to human sexuality to perspectives on history to values and ethics—*everything* has a spiritual element to it. Our kids will grow up seeing life through either a secular or a biblical lens. Every topic they cover will be impacted by the philosophy and theology of the person teaching it.

Even if it were possible to give our kids a neutral education, we as Christian parents are not called to do that. In the last point, I outlined a few Scriptures that undeniably point to our responsibility as parents to "train up our children" (Proverbs 22:6 and Ephesians 6:4, for starters). In addition, Deuteronomy chapters 6 and 11 offer a picture of family discipleship as an all-throughout-the-day (waking up, walking along the street, lying down, etc.) process.

As Christian parents, our job is not easy, but it is clear. And in the

Our children have developed a depth of character and faith that would be a challenge to develop in any other school environment.

world we live in today, it will not be possible to separate a child's education from their spiritual formation.

## Reason #11: "My Kids Have the Chance to Attend a Private Christian School"

If you have the means and live near a good, Bible-based private school, then it makes sense that you would consider that option. I have friends who are very happy with their experience in a private Christian school. I'm happy for them.

Before you jump in, however, I would suggest you do a few things:

- Look into the school's statement of belief and whether or not faculty sign a statement of faith. (Meet some teachers and ask them to share their testimony, if you can.)
- Find out school policies about cell phones, dress code, and anything else on your mind.
- Talk to families whose kids attend the school and ask questions about their experience at the school.
- Consider your child's readiness to handle peer pressure and whether they know what to do when exposed to pornographic or other inappropriate content.
- Look into spending a day at the school and sit in various classes as consider your options.
- Pray! Seek God's wisdom and trust him to lead you in this.

Keep in mind that sometimes a private Christian school attracts anyone who can afford to go there, which means regardless of what they are teaching, the peer culture is not a whole lot different from a public school. Be aware that cultural trends will find their way into even the best private school. Keep your eyes wide open.

If you do choose to send your child to a private school, I encourage you to be involved at the school wherever you can. Get to know the teachers and faculty, volunteer, and be intentional about conversations with your child about everything going on at school.

There will always be pros and cons. There is no school option that doesn't come with some drawbacks (homeschooling included). My personal opinion is that homeschooling is (still!) the very best option, but hey—I'm writing a homeschool book, so that shouldn't surprise you.

## How about You?

You may have obstacles or hesitations I have not listed, and I trust you will make the best decision for your family. No two families will have the same story, so don't fall into comparison or make choices for the wrong reasons. As you bring your family with all its uniqueness before the Lord, I am confident he will lead you. He will never steer you wrong because he loves your family very much.

As my husband and I earnestly considered and prayed about each of our initial concerns, it became clear to us that there was much more reason to give homeschooling a shot than to allow our fears to stop us. We may not have had all the answers yet, but facing those fears was the first step in our journey to becoming homeschoolers.

Reminder: You can find the link to the bonus chapter "Practical Help for Real Homeschool Challenges" in the resource section. Whether you are a single parent, are trying to homeschool multiple kids, or are struggling with monitoring screen time for your homeschooled kids, you'll discover encouragement there.

## TAKE-HOME THOUGHT
———

Most of the reasons people give for not homeschooling their kids do not compare to the blessings of working through the challenges of homeschooling.

## REFLECTION QUESTION
———

What has been your main reason not to homeschool, and what creative solutions might enable you to become a homeschooling family?

# GETTING STARTED

## 3 Simple Steps to Becoming Homeschoolers

When I asked people on social media for their biggest questions related to homeschooling, the most common response was "How do you get started?" Ah, yes. New things are scary! I remember well how, as soon as we decided to begin homeschooling, I found myself overwhelmed with questions and uncertainties. If you feel any of that, I am so glad you're here. Whatever age or grade your kids are, I hope this chapter gives you a strong foundation for homeschooling and a ton of assurance that you have what it takes.

The good news is, you really don't need a long on-ramp to begin homeschooling. It makes sense to begin at the start of a new school year, but there is no reason you can't pull a child out of school and start at any time. You can begin your homeschool journey whenever you want to.

In fact, there are only a few steps (I'm narrowing it down to three) to actually becoming homeschoolers. I'll cover them here, spending the bulk of this chapter on choosing a homeschooling style along with a curriculum. Then rest assured that you'll have many years ahead to figure out everything else. (And the remainder of this book will be a good guide for that.)

---

### Three Steps to Becoming Homeschoolers

1. Know the legal requirements to officially begin homeschooling.
2. Choose a homeschooling style and a curriculum.
3. Make a plan for how you want your homeschool days to look.

---

## Step 1: Know the Legal Requirements to Officially Begin Homeschooling

The first step to becoming homeschoolers is to become familiar with your state's legal requirements for homeschooling. If your child has been attending public school, you'll need to withdraw them properly. With a quick click on your home state at the Homeschool Legal Defense Association website (hslda.org/legal), you can learn how to properly withdraw from your public school and find the legal requirements to homeschool in your state. The HSLDA website has clear, current information for each state, including how to give your intent to homeschool, any required homeschool subjects, if and at what grade levels standardized testing is required, and more. You'll even find a video message given by an HSLDA attorney explaining the legal requirements for homeschooling in your state. HSLDA is a great resource you'll want to be acquainted with, and I have links to some of the most important pages on the HSLDA website in the resource section. For now, know that your state's specific page on the HSLDA website will be your go-to for all the legal aspects of homeschooling.

In the chapters ahead, we'll touch more on each stage of homeschooling and what should be on your radar. The only time there is a bit more to keep track of is if your kids are in high school. If you are just beginning to homeschool in high school, chapters 8 and 9 will guide you through the process with no sweat.

Now, go ahead and take a deep breath, because getting started is easy, and I'll be here for you every step of the way.

## Step 2: Choose a Homeschooling Style and a Curriculum

The second step to becoming homeschoolers will take a bit more time and thought. But hopefully you'll have fun with this step. It is choosing what to teach, or which "curriculum" you plan to use. Most of us stress over this step, but it is important to give yourself plenty of grace here. It is very normal to try a few (if not many) different curriculums during your homeschooling years.

I began the process of choosing curriculum eighteen years ago with the book *100 Top Picks for Homeschool Curriculum* by Cathy Duffy. This book still exists (in fact, there is now an updated *103 Top Picks* edition), and you can also go to Cathy Duffy's website to find updated curriculum reviews and more information.[1] *103 Top Picks* offers a framework to help you choose the best curriculum for your family based on your family's personal preferences, your teaching style, and your kids' learning styles. You can also find many similar helpful tools on various websites. (You'll find a few of my favorites in the resource list at the end of the book.)

When we first started homeschooling, I didn't spend much time analyzing learning styles or choosing curriculum. I simply talked to a few friends who were already homeschooling, did a little bit of research, and then ordered a curriculum that seemed to be a decent fit for our family. I knew I was unlikely to stick with what I'd ordered for the long term. I just knew I needed to get started. And I was right.

We really did enjoy what we used for that first year of homeschooling and even kept using it for the second year. But after that,

I switched things up. After talking to more homeschooling friends and exploring more options, I discovered a few things that worked well for my boys, as well as a few things that needed to be changed.

Changing things up—and not knowing exactly what you want at first—is very normal. Especially if your kids are young, you have a lot of time and freedom to explore different options. Some homeschool parents love the research process, and others are overwhelmed by it. I encourage you to do what's best for you and your family—mainly, don't stress out but enjoy the process.

In the resource section, you'll find a list of all the curriculums I used with my sons over the years, as well as a list of recommended curriculums for each subject level. This should give you a good starting point to begin choosing your own materials.

## A Brief Overview of Homeschooling Methods and Philosophies

If you are just learning about homeschooling, you may find it helpful and interesting to learn a bit about the main homeschooling methods or philosophies. If this information overwhelms you, feel free to come back to it later. Understanding all the types of homeschooling methods and philosophies is not essential when you get started (or ever, really).

> There are six main methods or styles of homeschooling: traditional, eclectic, Charlotte Mason, classical, unit studies, and unschooling.

When I began homeschooling, I had very little understanding of the different methods or interest in them, and I did just fine.

### Method 1: Traditional Homeschooling

Traditional homeschooling (some call this "school at home") most resembles a conventional school day, with a list of subjects to cover, reading and/or textbooks and workbooks (or something similar online), and quizzes, tests, and projects assigned. Often these come in an everything-you-need-in-one-box type of curriculum. This structure is familiar for most of us, especially new homeschoolers, and some parents and students thrive with this method. They enjoy completing workbooks and checking off their work as they go. (I relate!) Other homeschool families feel like this style would be stifling and defeat the purpose of homeschooling.

While similar in some ways to what a day at school might look like, using a traditional homeschooling approach offers many benefits. Because schoolwork is done at home, there is much more freedom in scheduling and environment. Parents who are thinking ahead to college requirements and feel most secure somewhat mirroring what a student would get in a typical school might feel most comfortable using the traditional method (at least when they're first starting out). I personally am drawn to this method of homeschooling.

### Method 2: Eclectic (or "Relaxed") Homeschooling

An eclectic (sometimes called "relaxed") homeschooling method is probably the most common approach used by the families who stick with homeschooling for the long run. Basically, eclectic homeschoolers do not adhere to one specific philosophy of homeschooling but choose what works best in the season they are in. Eclectic homeschoolers use a variety of resources—workbooks, videos, fiction and nonfiction books, hands-on projects—to create a school environment that is best for their children. It is common for eclectic homeschooling families to devote mornings to the core subjects and afternoons to "elective" or passion-led subjects, sports, internships, or other activities.

Once I got the hang of homeschooling, our homeschool method was somewhere between traditional and eclectic. Because

Dave and I hoped that our kids would go to college one day, we felt most secure making sure they were covering the topics that would be covered in a traditional school setting. But we also wanted to offer them the chance to explore their interests and, of course, to pursue sports and activities outside the home.

Most families who practice an eclectic style of homeschooling follow a somewhat typical curriculum plan for their child's grade level. For example, I had my boys do a state history class the same year the public schools did. It is also common for both traditional and eclectic homeschoolers to administer standardized tests for their students each year. Annual tests can help kids get practice for the bigger (SAT or ACT) tests they are likely to take later, and they can also give parents an idea of their progress. Note, however, that some students may be very bright—and even excellent students—yet not do well on standardized tests. If you find that testing is more stressful than beneficial, I would encourage you to consider skipping it (at least some years). Remember, you get to choose what is best for your unique children.

### Method 3: Charlotte Mason

The Charlotte Mason method is one I've always admired. Charlotte Mason was an author, educator, and speaker who emphasized teaching the whole child with quality literature (also called *living books*), nature study, art, and hands-on projects. Her method makes learning a way of life rather than a task to be done. Charlotte Mason homeschooling is really a lifestyle—one focused on nature, reading, and a lot of conversation between parent and child. Those who follow a Charlotte Mason approach typically use dictation, journaling, and a lot of copy work.

Charlotte Mason believed that children should be given ample time to explore, create, play, and learn from real-life situations. Families who use a Charlotte Mason approach like to take field trips to museums and art galleries and might be found traveling the world with a sketchpad and journal. (Doesn't it sound dreamy? If I had one more child to homeschool, maybe I'd try this method.)

There are many wonderful Charlotte Mason quotes, but a simple one that perhaps best defines her philosophy is this: "Education is an atmosphere, a discipline, a life."[2] I list some helpful resources for each method of homeschooling at the back of the book, but a couple of popular books on this method include *A Charlotte Mason Education: A Home Schooling How-To Manual* and *More Charlotte Mason Education: A Home Schooling How-To Manual*, both by Catherine Levison.

### Method 4: Classical

The classical homeschooling method goes back the farthest (apparently way back to the Middle Ages!) and is associated with many great minds of history. Classical homeschooling aims to train students to become learners and is based on the trivium, which uses the developmental stages children progress through—grammar, logic, and rhetoric—as its foundation. The Classical Conversations website explains the trivium this way: "Consider a simple analogy to understand the Trivium arts before we explore them in more detail: grammar is the inputting of data, dialectic is the processing of data, and rhetoric is the outputting of data."[3]

To give you an idea of how this might work, let's take the example of studying the World War II attack on Pearl Harbor (keeping things close to my home).

In the *grammar* stage (grades K–5), kids would learn all about the attack on Pearl Harbor. This would include all the names, dates, and other facts that were an important part of the event.

In the *logic* stage (grades 6–8), students would take all the information they learned in the grammar stage and begin to ask "how" and "why" questions: What led to the attack on Pearl Harbor?

Why Pearl Harbor? How did the attack lead to the US entering World War II? Taking time to discuss, read, and write in response to these questions brings clarity and more understanding of the facts learned about the attack on Pearl Harbor.

Finally, in the *rhetoric* stage (grades 9–12), students would integrate the grammar and logic stages with more mature conversations and understanding. Students might explore other historical events with patterns similar to Pearl Harbor. They might consider how the attack affected things that are a part of their lives today. During the rhetoric stage, students often do more in-depth writing projects, tackle persuasive speaking assignments, and engage in higher-level reading. The goal is to gain wisdom from the topic and apply that wisdom to life today.

All three of these phases—grammar, logic, and rhetoric—are used to teach students how to learn. Classically educated kids are taught to be disciplined and to have an overall appreciation for education. There is a lot to love about this method. A popular book on the classical approach is *The Well-Trained Mind: A Guide to Classical Education at Home* by Susan Wise Bauer and Jessie Wise.

### Method 5: Unit Studies

The unit studies method of homeschooling uses themes to cover many topics—for a variety of ages—at the same time. Families may choose units based on a child's interests, or they might purchase a boxed curriculum that has a series of units prepared for them. Themes range from studying specific plants or animals to historical themes or figures, to geography (such as oceans and mountain ranges), science (astronomy, electricity, or marine biology), and more. Typically, a family will choose a theme, then spend several weeks reading a book on the theme, doing hands-on activities, taking field trips, working on writing projects, and more—all based on that theme. A student might do their math separately (or, in the early years, math might be incorporated into the unit theme), with everything else done as part of the unit. Unit studies can be especially great for families who have more than one child who are close in age (just a few grade levels apart), as everyone can do the same basic unit study, with the parent adjusting assignments to fit each child's grade level.

Some eclectic homeschooling families might take a break from their typical studies to do a unit study for the month of December, or they might do a unit study related to a current event (the Olympics or a presidential election, for example). Unit studies can be a fun way to do school in the summer as well. When my boys were young, we once took a break from normal "school" and did an Advent unit for the month of December. We also did a casual unit study one summer while planting our vegetable garden. These are some of my favorite homeschool memories.

### Method 6: Unschooling

Families who use the unschooling method embrace the freedom of homeschooling. Unschoolers have confidence that children will learn naturally when they are not tied to a specific curriculum, though they often fill their days with a lot of learning through books, nature, and other passion-led explorations.

Some homeschool experts suggest that unschooling is a great way to transition from a conventional school to homeschooling, as it is so different that it can't help but force you to switch gears. I admire families who enjoy an unschooling lifestyle, even though I don't think it would be a great fit for my personality.[4] However, I can imagine certain seasons of life when using an unschooling method would be refreshing for the students—and probably more educational than I would have imagined.

## You Get to Choose

After reading over these main methods of homeschooling (or taking an online assessment, which you can find links to in the resource section), you might have quickly identified a method of homeschooling that you think would be best for your family. However, don't worry if you end up trying a few different ones before you land on the best fit. (And it's not unusual to end up using different styles for different kids.) Your children may go through various stages that nudge you to branch out and try something new. Most of us end up incorporating a good mix of styles, which becomes our very own "method" of homeschooling. That's totally fine!

## Learning Styles

The better you know and understand your children, the better you will be able to customize their education according to their unique learning style. I like to talk about being a "student of your students," observing both what lights them up and what frustrates them. You might already have some ideas about how they learn from simply observing them.

> The better you know and understand your children, the better you will be able to customize their education according to their unique learning style.

When I noticed my oldest son's eagerness to carry his dad's medical textbooks with him at a young age, I recognized his love of learning and desire to learn everything possible. When I spotted my second son's fascination with how things work—taking apart a toy or alarm clock, tinkering with machines whenever he got the chance—I was given a hint of his engineering brain. My third son has been social from a young age and is motivated by working with others. My youngest son loves music, and his brain is stimulated if I allow him to listen to music while he does school. These simple observations offered me a lot of direction for homeschooling them as individuals.

It is also helpful to consider your personal preference as the homeschool teacher (or "facilitator," as I call myself since my boys have become more independent). Do you enjoy (and have time for) being involved in your child's entire school day, or do you prefer to use some video lessons, outside instructors, co-op classes, or other resources?

Asking yourself a few more questions can help you narrow down your curriculum choice:

- How much can I budget for homeschool curriculum?
- Do I want an all-in-one curriculum, or do I prefer à la carte resources?
- Would I like to use a Christian/Bible-based curriculum?
- Is it important to me to offer my children multisensory resources?
- Do I want to use a parent-led curriculum, or are my kids ready for more independent learning?
- Do I want/need to use an "accredited" curriculum?

### Costly Curriculum or on a Budget?

How much you spend on a curriculum is up to you. Some families go all out, while others make things work on a very tight budget. Most years I spent close to $1,000 per student on the entire year's homeschool curriculum. (Fees for sports and outside clubs or activities were in addition to that.) The younger boys were able to use some hand-me-down books and supplies from the older brothers, so that saved us some money over time. With some creativity (and a good local library), you can make things work on much less than I spent. I have friends who homeschool their kids for under $100 each by using free online resources, the library, and hand-me-downs from friends.

### All-in-One Curriculum or à la Carte Resources?

An all-in-one (sometimes called "boxed") curriculum includes everything you need for all the subjects for a whole year. I love these for the sake of not worrying that I have missed something. However, as my boys grew older and we figured out what worked best for them (and for our family), I ended up choosing from a few different curriculums each year. If you prefer to pick and choose the materials you use from subject to subject, consider a curriculum (or several different curriculums) that allows resources to be purchased separately, or à la carte.

### Christian Curriculum or Secular?

If discipleship and biblical worldview foundations are part of your goals and reason for homeschooling, then Christian curriculum resources will support you in your approach. There are many great Christian as well as secular curriculums available, whether you're looking for something rigorous and college-preparatory or something more relaxed.

### Book-Based or Multisensory?

Multisensory resources are great for kids who learn best using their five senses. For example, one of my boys understood math best using hands-on tools for place value. Some kids learn best by doing, while others might be just fine reading information in a book or listening to a teacher online.

### Parent-Led or Independent Learning?

Parent-led curriculums are designed to be taught to each child, while resources for independent learning are given either directly to the child for learning (in the form of textbooks or workbooks) or through video lessons or a web-based curriculum.

If you choose a parent-led approach to homeschooling, you will need to be available to teach lessons using a teacher's manual, answer keys, and other resources. This method is often used during the early years or for children with unique learning needs.

Independent learning resources put more of the responsibility on children for their own education. Kids learn from a video or books, and the parent (or homeschool facilitator) is available to grade or evaluate work and to give help when needed. Independent learning curriculums are great for large families and are often used more as students hit the high school years.

### Accredited or Unaccredited Curriculums?

Often people looking into homeschooling ask me about home-school "accreditation." Is it necessary to use an "accredited" program? This can get confusing, so I'll do my best to keep it simple: accreditation is a form of credentialing that applies to academic institutions (brick-and-mortar schools). This means that a homeschool program, by nature, *cannot be accredited*. If you are searching for an accredited homeschool program, you are likely to come across online or virtual schools, not just a homeschool curriculum.[5]

The nuance of using an accredited school is that students work directly with a teacher (virtually), turn in their work to the school, and receive grades from the school. This means that students must be on the school's academic calendar.

Some homeschool curriculums offer both independent home-schooling and an "accredited" option. For example, my boys used the Abeka curriculum for many of their classes. They watched lectures on video, then did bookwork and took quizzes and tests, which I corrected and graded. We were fully independent. However, Abeka also offers the Abeka Academy accredited program. If we had opted for this version, it would have cost more money, but the boys would have worked with a teacher (online) and received grades from the virtual academy. If a student uses an accredited program for all their classes, they will also receive a transcript from that program at the end of twelfth grade, which looks similar to a private school transcript.

We have never used an accredited program, and I think in most cases it is not necessary or sufficiently advantageous to make it worth the extra cost and loss of freedom. However, if a parent works full-time, doesn't want to grade schoolwork, or doesn't feel comfortable creating a high school transcript (though it's not hard, and we'll get to that in chapter 8), then an accredited program is worth looking into. There are many good ones out there, both faith-based and secular, and you can find links to them in the resource section.

Freedom is one of the greatest blessings of becoming homeschoolers.

Your own family's homeschool experience will vary greatly depending on the method and curriculum you choose. The great news is, you can always switch things up. Once we invested in a curriculum, we tried to stick with it for an entire school year, though there were times we ditched a curriculum midyear and ordered something new. Don't worry if the same thing happens to you. Just keep in mind that freedom is one of the greatest blessings of becoming homeschoolers.

## Step 3: Make a Plan for How You Want Your Homeschool Days to Look

Once you've found out the legal requirements to homeschool and decided on a method and curriculum that might work for your family, it's time to create at least a loose plan for getting started.

## Using a Homeschool Planner

Many homeschooling families use a homeschool planner, though I have yet to try one. (I provide some links to favorites in the resource section, and who knows if I might just try one myself.) You can simply use a regular calendar to organize a plan for your first days and months of homeschooling.

## Create at Least a Loose Schedule

Whether or not you personally thrive with an organized schedule, most kids do. I recommend writing out a plan for how you might organize your homeschool days. Leave lots of wiggle room for the unexpected. Also consider throwing some extra fun into the plan—especially if you have some hesitant new homeschoolers. We will go further into creating a daily (and weekly and beyond) schedule, and I'll share a homeschool "day in the life" from our family in chapter 13.

## Find Your People

No parent should have to take on the responsibility of training and raising their children without adequate support from family, friends, a church community, and mentors. While having family that supports and validates your choice to homeschool is valuable, you will also want friends who share the homeschool experience with you and your kids. These friends can offer advice and encouragement based on personal experience, and you can have fun traveling the homeschool journey together. Homeschool co-ops are another great way to team up with other homeschooling families. (We'll talk more about co-ops in chapter 12.)

Homeschooling families often come together online on social media or as followers of homeschool bloggers. Search Facebook or other places on the internet for like-minded homeschool communities to join and collaborate with.

## Homeschool Conventions

Homeschool conventions can be a great way to find inspiration, learn new methods of teaching, and discover new curriculums. They're also a place to meet fellow homeschooling families. When my boys were young, I faithfully attended a homeschool convention in Honolulu. While I would enter each year feeling uncertain and unqualified (imposter syndrome, anyone?), I always left feeling inspired and encouraged (and usually with a bunch of fun resources I impulse-purchased in the conventional hall). Homeschool conventions are usually large events that happen once a year in certain states or regions. I include a list of popular conventions in the resource section, but two that are always excellent are the Teach Them Diligently convention and the Great Homeschool Conventions, both of which meet in various cities across the United States.

# New Things Are Scary, but...

If you are just stepping into this world of homeschooling—either with excitement or with trepidation (or both!)—rest assured, you are not alone. Like I said at the start of this chapter, new things are scary. But I also want to remind you that everything you've ever done was once a "new thing." Getting dressed. Making pancakes. Driving a car. (Remember how scary that once seemed?) As I have often said, "You have to be bad at things before you get good at them!" As hard as learning new things is, nothing is worse than the regret of not trying and wishing you had, right?

Similarly, learning to homeschool is not easy, but I encourage you to take it all in stride. I never felt like the homeschool mom who had it all together, and yet somehow I've graduated three kids from high school. I've tried hard, made a lot of mistakes, and gone through seasons when I homeschooled through burnout. The good news is, my kids did just fine in every season. And I went from feeling like I was not good at homeschooling to, well, writing an entire book about it!

I'll never forget one especially rough day early on in my homeschool journey when I called a friend and confessed that I didn't feel like I was cut out to be a homeschool mom. In fact, I felt like a failure. I was sure my boys would be better off learning at a "real school" than in my home. My friend said to me, "Your worst homeschool day gives your kids more than they would get in their best day in a public school." She didn't have any data to back that up, but I didn't need it. Deep down, I knew that giving my kids a happy, healthy, safe home to live and learn in was the greatest gift I could give them. So I pressed on.

The truth is, I have repeated my friend's words to myself many times since, because even now I sometimes struggle to feel qualified to be a homeschool mom. Remembering that God didn't call me to be perfect, just to be faithful, resets my perspective every time. And his grace will always be enough. I often remind myself of 2 Corinthians 9:8: "God is able to bless you abundantly, so that in all things at all times, having all that you need, you will abound in every good work."

## TAKE-HOME THOUGHT

The first step is always the hardest, and homeschooling is no exception; but there is so much good ahead if you are willing to give it a try.

## REFLECTION QUESTION

What do you need to learn or do to take your next step toward becoming homeschoolers?

PART II

PRESCHOOL
TO COLLEGE

CHAPTER 5

# CURIOUS AND CUDDLY

## Homeschooling Preschool

Many people say that the easiest time to begin homeschooling is from the very start. In the natural progression from baby to toddler to preschool years, a child's brain is rapidly developing, and huge amounts of learning are happening without any formal education. The preschool years are many parents' favorite time to teach their kids, and incredible bonds can be established between parents and children in these sweet, early years. I can't imagine a better time to begin homeschooling your kids than during the preschool years.

With that being said, I will confess: I sent all my boys to preschool. *Outside of my house.* In other words, I did not homeschool preschool (gasp!).

It's a little strange to write that or even to think back on it. Sending my boys to preschool seemed so normal, and necessary, to me at the time, but if I could go back, I would probably do things differently.

As I shared earlier, my first two sons went to preschool before

> The preschool years are many parents' favorite time to teach their kids.

homeschooling was even on my radar. They attended a private Christian school where they sat at desks, had a structured schedule, wore a uniform, and were expected to meet very high standards (for preschool). There was honestly a lot I liked about that, especially the fact that it taught them a lot of discipline. This was helpful as we transitioned to homeschooling, because their only association with "school" was so structured that I think they were less inclined to be wild or to misbehave during our (home) "school days."

By the time our fourth son, Levi, was preschool age, we had moved to the country and were a good distance from the preschool his older brothers had gone to. I was homeschooling my older three boys—ages thirteen, eleven, and nine at the time—and I had begun my online writing career. I was also in my forties, and though that may not be completely relevant, I was feeling stretched and more exhausted than ten years earlier when my first boys were in preschool. (Fair enough?)

I signed Levi up for a part-time program at a local Christian church preschool, which was much more relaxed than his older brothers' school had been. The teachers were all sweet, but it seemed a bit more like daycare than "school." And Levi hated it. He resisted going—*to the point of tears*—almost every single day.

I don't like thinking about it now, but at the time I reasoned that it was good for him to go even though he didn't want to. I believed that he just didn't like having to go to school when he knew his brothers were doing school at home (which was probably true). He was unable to communicate well at three years old, so I may never know why he disliked preschool so much. But I kept sending him, telling myself he would eventually learn to like it—and believing that I needed the break. Also, I planned to homeschool him in a year or two, so I hoped the time spent in preschool might prepare him for that.

On the positive side, I was glad that Levi was able to do some of the messy crafts at preschool that I didn't want to do at home. (I've never been a big fan of glue and glitter!) His teachers read Bible stories aloud, he got to do some water play, and he learned how to get along with other kids on the playground. He was introduced to a lot of different students, and he learned to wait in lines, eat a sack lunch, and lie still for nap hour (which he still recalls being torturous). He also caught a lot of viruses, and one month he brought home head lice. *Twice.*

Even as I write this, I feel a little bad about that whole experience. I mean, he was safe, and I don't think I was being evil by sending him to preschool, but I do think I was being a little selfish. I am sure there were creative solutions I could have implemented in that season that might have been better for Levi. Regardless, it all worked out okay. Levi and his big brothers all survived preschool and transitioned to homeschooling just fine.

In light of that story, I want to acknowledge, again, that every family needs to figure out what is best for them in the season they are in. Sending a child to preschool may be a good option for your family for a variety of reasons. As long as you do your due diligence and check out the preschool situation well—including the teachers, the curriculum, and the policies for whom your child is with at various times (for things like bathroom visits)—a season at preschool may not be the worst thing for your child. And in some cases, it might be great. But then again, homeschooling preschool might be even better. So let's talk about that.

## If You Choose to Homeschool Preschool . . .

Preschool is not currently mandated by law, so you have a lot of freedom when homeschooling preschool! It can be an ideal time to ease into educating your kids without the stress of legal requirements. Though they have already been absorbing heaps of information into their rapidly growing brains, by the time kids are three or four years old, they are often ready to begin learning with a little more structure. And there is no doubt that these can be some fun years!

I struggled with a wide-open day and no set schedule when my boys were young. Homeschooling allows us to have a bit of order to our days and offers kids the structure and predictability they need as well. Loosely organizing days around "school," play, rest, and so on can be helpful.

## Curriculum

You will find many preschool curriculums available, and many are very good. Using a curriculum might help you get an idea of what is normal to cover in each subject and will also prepare you for the kind of organization and planning you'll need in the years ahead. However, a curriculum is not at all necessary at this age. If you feel comfortable doing your own thing, do it! You have many more years ahead to follow academic curriculums if you want to.

## School "Spaces"

A quick look at Pinterest or at a creative homeschool mom's social media account can make you think you need to set up a dedicated classroom or homeschool space, but that is not true. If you have the space and resources, it might be fun to do so (especially if you have more children and plan to homeschool for the long term), but it is definitely not necessary. Preschool kids love to snuggle with a book on the couch, color at the kitchen counter, and take a blanket outside to spend time in nature.

If you start off too complicated or set your expectations too high, burnout is likely. I had one friend who—when her kids were in preschool—began her homeschool journey by choosing to be up and dressed in what she felt was professional teacher attire, in their dedicated classroom, by 8:00 a.m., five days a week. She was determined to "teach" up to par with what she remembered from her own private school experience. I wasn't too surprised when that friend gave up homeschooling before her kids had completed a full year of preschool. Keep in mind: order, spaces, and schedule are meant to bring sanity, not stress!

### What to Teach Preschoolers

A fellow boy-mom friend of mine tells her sons, "It is my job to work; your job is to play!" I love that! (Though she confesses it backfired when her too-smart seven-year-old resisted his chores, saying, "Sorry, Mom, I'm just busy doing my job!")

Kids learn through playing, and they will naturally play if you let them! The best thing you can give your three- and four-year-olds is a lot of time to run, climb, explore, and . . . even to be bored. Yes, I am a big believer in giving kids that white space of boredom to get curious and create, to think and wonder and ask questions.

> I am a big believer in giving kids that white space of boredom to get curious and create, to think and wonder and ask questions.

Children today lack the opportunity to be bored, partly due to (well-intentioned) parents keeping them always busy doing exciting things and partly due to technology (which is increasingly often the "exciting thing"). I have heard it said that "boredom is the gateway to creativity." And yes! I've seen it myself a thousand times: in bored-stiff moments, my older boys (the ones who were kids before smartphones and all the devices were everywhere) did some crazy (cool) stuff. I recall masterpieces made with paper and glue, expansive blanket forts housing wild (stuffed) animals and snacks, and countless hours of imaginary play. They opened books they didn't think they'd like (only to discover they actually liked them) and designed an underwater hotel. (That still begs to be built, Josiah!)

Preschool kids are naturally eager to learn, and you can begin to teach them through a lot of simple, hands-on activities. You might set up stations in your home or yard (in Hawaii, we did a lot in our garage!) focusing on different "subjects." A corner of the house dedicated to books is one of the best things you can provide for your preschooler (along with many trips to the library). You might consider a science area equipped with anything from an aquarium to a sand or water table, a children's microscope, or a bin full of toy animals or rocks. One of my sons asked for a play grocery store for his third birthday, and while playing "checker," we would talk about fruits and veggies and healthy foods and "treats," as well as customer service and money. You can set up an art table with paper, crayons, and basic art supplies. Dress-up bins are great for developing the imagination and learning about other cultures, jobs, or characters. A dollhouse or workbench can provide hours of creative play for preschoolers. (My dad built my boys a simple workbench to go in the garage next to where their daddy did projects.) The list of learning "toy" options goes on and on, and most of these items can be simple, homemade, hand-me-downs, or thrifted.

### Get Outside!

One of the greatest gifts you can give to your preschooler is lots of time outside. A fenced-in yard can entertain a curious kid for hours every day. I have great memories (and some hilarious photos) of my sons naked in our fenced-in yard, using paintbrushes to decorate our wood fence with watercolor paints. They caught geckos and other critters, looked for frogs, and on hot days played in our tiny blow-up swimming pool. As they got a little bit older, their imaginations became their greatest pastime as they made up stories together about adventures and bad guys and heroes. If you live where there are seasons, suiting your kids up with a rain jacket and galoshes or a snowsuit and boots can make for great fun in all kinds of weather. Dave and I grew up in the Pacific Northwest, and we both remember outdoor play year-round.

I write all this with a nostalgic smile on my face as I recall those early years with preschool boys, but no doubt it wasn't always sweet and dreamy in the moment. The days can be very, very long, and kids are not always content to play quietly, explore their yard, or get along with their siblings. You may not be able to get outside for a variety of reasons, and too many hours with preschool-age children might make you feel a bit crazy. I understand.

A bit of structure can be very helpful during the preschool years. So can trips to the park, visits to a children's museum, or an annual pass to the local zoo.

## Subjects to Cover

If you feel ready to begin a "school routine," consider a loose schedule to plan your days around. While there are countless options for all that you can introduce your preschooler to, it might be helpful to decide on a few subjects to incorporate into your daily schedule.

### Bible Devotions

There is no better way to start the day than with Bible reading and prayer. Dave and I begin every day this way, and I have always *tried* to be up before the kids so I can spend time alone with God in the mornings. When the kids were young, they would get up and curl up next to me for a simple time of reading a children's Bible and devotional and praying. This is a daily discipline that we have made a priority through the years, and I am so glad that my adult sons continue to make devotional time with God a part of their independent lives.

## Reading

Reading out loud is probably the most important "school" subject you can do with your preschooler. Kids love this special time with their parents, and countless good books for the early years are available. The local library can be your best friend during these years, and preschool kids love the process of picking out a big stack of books to check out and pore over at home. (I don't want to talk about the late fees I've paid over the years at our public library, but you can do better than me, I'm sure.)

Preschoolers have short attention spans, so I recommend you read aloud for short periods of time throughout the day. Picture books are wonderful, and kids love to take their time studying each page and talking through the story as you read. And they also love repetition. Preschool kids often want to read their favorite books over and over. And over and over. That's good for their brains, so just go with it. By the time Jonah was through preschool, I could "read" *Goodnight Moon* without even looking at the words. With that in mind, it is wise to choose books you enjoy (or at least can tolerate), because you might just be stuck with them for a week (or fifty-two).

As you read to your child, you can begin to point out letters and sounds. "Look at the big balloon! *B* says *buh*. . . ." This is the beginning of phonics. It's really exciting when you realize you are doing "school" in the comfort of your pj's on the couch!

## Math

As with reading, you can begin to teach math concepts without any formal curriculum. Number recognition in the books you read—and all around the house, grocery store, and anywhere else you go—can be fun and natural. You can also count things for fun—fingers and toes, items on a plate, toys lined up, and just about anything else!

Some kids will be more drawn to mathematical concepts than others, so take note! If your child loves numbers, you might enjoy experimenting to see how much they are ready to understand. Cheer and celebrate when they count on their own, add one plus one, or notice that there are four people (plus one dog and one cat!) in the family. I don't think I can overemphasize that math for preschoolers can and should be *fun*!

The more you are simply aware—looking around at all the available learning tools in your everyday life—the easier and more fun the early learning years will be. This applies not just to math but to any other "subject." Your kids will follow your lead, and soon your preschooler will be noticing and pointing out many wonderful things in their home, in nature, and all around them!

### Calendar Time

Many of the things taught in a traditional preschool are practical— the days of the week, months of the year, seasons, weather, and basic routines. You might add a short time at the end of your Bible devotions in the morning when you talk about all these things. You can find creative calendars and hands-on materials for making these daily routines entertaining and memorable. If you're the creative type, you can design your own calendar and materials!

### Phonics

If you are reading aloud plenty, phonics will be a natural next step. Like I said earlier, you can begin by pointing out letters and sounds, but at some point you might want to teach phonics with a bit more structure. A quick online search will give you plenty of teaching materials to consider (and might even overwhelm you), but simple flashcards with letters and sounds, some coloring printables, or a basic book for learning phonics should give you plenty to work with. There are a lot of online games that teach phonics as well, although if you use those, I'd reserve them for playtime rather than use them as your main lesson.

### Colors, Shapes, and Art

Preschoolers' brains are like sponges, and if you are truly eager to teach, learning can happen all day long and without much more than what you already have in your natural surroundings. With a box of crayons and some paper, you can introduce your child to colors and inspire a love of art at the same time.

Sidewalk chalk, watercolors, and coloring books are some of the most wonderful tools for raising—and teaching—preschoolers. I have many fond memories of coloring with my boys, especially when they were sick or had a broken leg or were stuck indoors during a rainstorm. In fact, experts have told us how good coloring is for us as adults. If you're feeling stressed, coloring with your preschooler will do you both a lot of good!

As you go about your day, you can also point out colors, shapes, and textures all around you. Notice that a car's wheels are round, a building might be a square or a rectangle, the kitty's nose is a triangle. The sky might be blue and the trees are so green. Oh, parents, if you have the privilege of homeschooling a preschooler, I hope you soak in all of God's goodness in creation right alongside them!

If you have the privilege of homeschooling a preschooler, I hope you soak in all of God's goodness in creation right alongside them!

### Fine and Gross Motor Skills

Preschool-age kids are naturally wired to develop coordination, strength, and so many other motor skills. Playtime, especially outdoors where there is a lot of space to move, is great for this, and you can encourage even more movement by providing them with a mini-trampoline to jump on, balls, and other play or sports equipment. Some kids love early gymnastics or dance classes, and I'm a fan of starting kids swimming as early as possible. For fine motor skills, we can help our kids learn to write (holding a pen or pencil properly takes some training!), sort small objects (putting silverware away is great practice), and use children's scissors. All these things can be incorporated into the natural rhythms of play and our household tasks, and kids will be developing important skills without even realizing it.

## Social Studies, Science, History, and Logical Thinking

While preschool is a bit young to teach many topics in a structured way, it is not a bad idea to have a variety of subjects on your mind. Laying a foundation for understanding other cultures, seasons and cycles in nature, how maps and globes work, and cause and effect can all be taught by talking about them naturally as you read stories together and go through your day. When you notice that your child has specific questions or interests, you can dive in and discover more together.

## Character Development

Perhaps one of the greatest opportunities you have with your preschooler is to begin to shape their heart and character. If not earlier, by age three or four these little humans display a sin nature. No one needs to teach your preschooler how to say no, throw a fit, or hit their sibling. We parents get the joyful job of teaching them good character. And yes, I say "joyful" with a little sarcasm, but I truly have learned that teaching little ones to be good citizens can be a lot of fun!

> One of the greatest opportunities you have with your preschooler is to begin to shape their heart and character.

Teaching character when kids are little is mostly about behavior, manners, and habits. You should teach them to say please and thank you, to obey quickly, and to help and share. You can instruct them on how to interrupt properly and explain how they can use self-control when they are frustrated (which, you have probably learned, can happen often in the preschool years).

Character development is one of the greatest opportunities of homeschooling in the early years. Parents, we have the chance to shape and mold these young hearts all day every day—when we read Bible stories and eat meals and even while we stack blocks one on top of the next. Bringing "character words" into all the little things we do helps kids wrap their growing minds around big concepts like patience, kindness, perseverance, and honesty.

Our culture is seeing the fruit of a generation of parents who often coddled and overprotected their kids—physically and emotionally. These kids are now discovering that in the real world not everyone gets a medal just for showing up, and expressing all your feelings all the time is not always healthy and is often a big mistake. A lot of young adults today are struggling with the concept of hard work and personal ownership, and we can learn a lesson from how they got there.

As homeschool parents, we can teach our kids the biblical principles of doing all things with excellence, of being faithful and loyal, even when there is a cost. We must teach our kids that love is patient and kind, and it is not proud. These concepts are taught and caught, and homeschool parents have a high calling both to teach and model.

I am convinced that if homeschool parents can do this one important job of developing character in their children, they will be giving them a gift that will bring blessings into their lives (not to mention those around them) for the rest of their lives. Start character development lessons young, and keep them going through the entirety of your homeschooling.

P.S.: On this topic of character, find a link in the resource section to my Character Training Course, which I open a few times a year. This online, self-paced course has helped parents all over the world raise kids of godly character.

### Field Trips

Field trip opportunities to explore with your preschooler abound. A day at a zoo or aquarium, a visit to a local museum (if it caters to children), or a simple wander through a garden or park can be remarkably educational for kids. Anytime you are out and about, you can put on your "teacher hat" and consider creative ways to add some learning to the day. You can take a walk and pick up leaves to bring home and study (or rub over as an art project), find shells at a beach, watch birds at the park, or stargaze at night. There are many ways for families to naturally teach preschoolers and to make memories doing it!

## What Preschoolers Need Most

Often by the time you have a preschooler, you also have a baby in the house—or perhaps on the way. You might be becoming home-schoolers with a preschooler as well as older kids (in or out of school), or you might be working from home or caring for an aging parent or a child with special needs. All this talk about savoring your days and field trips might sound nice, but in your case, it's less than realistic.

Please don't stress about this.

Your preschooler does not *need* full days of nature, education, and stimulation to grow up with a healthy brain and body. But they do need some! So come up with a schedule that is reasonable—and doable. A typical preschool is often only half a day, and part of that time includes free play, snacks, bathroom breaks, and sometimes even a nap. Can you commit two hours of your day (broken up, per-haps) to intentionally focused time with your preschooler? After that you might give them a bin of toys, a container of playdough, plenty of books, and time with their siblings, grandparents, or even your friendly family dog, and they will do just fine. If you give your preschooler a safe and loving home, healthy food, and the freedom to play and learn, you are giving them a truly amazing start to their education.

> If you give your preschooler a safe and loving home, healthy food, and the freedom to play and learn, you are giving them a truly amazing start to their education.

During their preschool years, you want to help your child build a foundation of letters and numbers, concepts, colors, and character qualities. Your child will be transforming, before your very eyes, from a carefree tot to a unique little person who has real questions and interests and dreams. What a joy that you get to be the shepherd—the guide for this beautiful preschool experience. Yes, your preschooler needs to learn structure and routine. They need to learn to be gentle and thoughtful. But most of all, they need to know they are loved by God and safe with their family in an environment where they are free to play, grow, and develop. Enjoy this season of homeschooling your precious preschooler.

## TAKE-HOME THOUGHT

Homeschooling your preschooler is likely to become one of your favorite parenting memories.

## REFLECTION QUESTION

Where can you adjust your perspective to see the preschool years as a chance to shape a little life and set a foundation for your child's amazing potential?

CHAPTER 6

# MAGICAL AND MISCHIEVOUS

## Homeschooling Elementary School

I've heard many parents say they intend to homeschool "eventually" but plan to send their kids to a public elementary school while things are still "pretty tame." "Then," they often add, "I'll homeschool when they hit middle or high school to avoid all the negatives that arise with increasing peer pressure and political agendas."

This sounds great *in theory*. But you likely agree with me that this theory does not hold up to reality anymore. Elementary school is no longer "tame" in many places. Rather, it is a target. More and more, we are seeing evidence of cultural indoctrination of children at younger and younger ages. *Primarily in public schools.*

Even before kids step into the classroom or onto the playground, many of them are carrying technology in their pockets and backpacks (or at least have access to it in their homes). Devices may have become normalized in our culture (they can be a very good babysitter—I get that), but we must be aware of the danger lurking on the other side of those screens. Danger that can be passed on to other kids on a school bus or on the playground.

It is not unusual for elementary school kids to introduce themselves with and discuss their gender pronouns. The average age for boys to be exposed to pornography is now nine years old. Younger and younger kids are dealing with anxiety and depression, and, sadly, more and more elementary students are even attempting suicide. I wish I were exaggerating all these facts, but I am not.

Each thing I just listed (along with many more concerns) is a cultural issue that is passed along through peers and schoolmates. There is no doubt—elementary-age kids are incredibly vulnerable, and we must take seriously our job to protect them.

## The Truth about Homeschooling in the Elementary Years

When I first considered homeschooling, I remember thinking it might be wise to start young so I'd have a few years to get my footing—to find what worked and what didn't. I said to my husband, "I probably can't mess up first grade too much. But ninth or tenth grade might be a different story." I had been warned that the first few years of homeschooling can be challenging, especially if your kids were transitioning from a traditional school setting. I had been told it wasn't unusual to shed a few tears (sometimes daily) in those first few years. But I was also told that the elementary years were magical—full of imagination, exploration, and wonder.

*And all of it was true.*

My first few years of homeschooling *were* challenging. I did make a lot of mistakes. And yes, I cried a lot. But I also couldn't believe how much I loved our new homeschooling life. It was a whole mix of things.

I am glad we started young, because by the time my boys were in their more serious and rigorous academic years, I was much more confident in my ability to homeschool and ready to face the challenges of teaching different subjects. But maybe more than anything, I'm glad I started early, because it is those sweet early years I absolutely treasure in my memory. Nothing compares to the *aha* moments shared with an elementary student!

But how do we get started homeschooling kids in this stage? What do our elementary-age children need to learn? What should we plan to teach them? Since there is a lot of development happening in the elementary years, I will divide this stage into two levels—early elementary and upper elementary—to cover the most important things.

## Early Elementary Years (Grades K-3)

The early elementary years have the potential to be very exciting! Especially if you do not have older kids with more demanding schedules, these years provide you with freedom to teach and learn without the stress that will naturally come as your kids get older.

Children in kindergarten through third grade often enjoy learning and are excited about school—unless you overdo it or set your expectations of them too high. A lot of kids really love learning to read and doing simple math, and there is nothing better than seeing the light bulb moments when they learn a new concept or master a skill. A favorite part of homeschooling for me has been when something really "clicks" with one of my boys and they forget that they are doing school at all, such as when Josiah created a notebook filled with sketches (one of the human heart and others of flying cars and other futuristic machines). Or when Levi started gathering facts about the solar system on a small sketchpad and taped them into a notebook. Instead of moving on to the next "subject" in school, homeschooling allowed them the freedom to keep following those passions in a natural ("homeschool-y") way.

## Curriculum

Choosing curriculum in the early elementary years can feel overwhelming, but what you must keep in mind is that you have freedom to try different things—and to switch it up if you aren't loving it. Remember, you do not have to use a formal curriculum at all yet. Plenty of families enjoy using books, free online resources, coloring sheets, and other creative approaches to schooling in these early years.

Yes, you'll want to explore your options and talk to friends who have gone before you. But eventually you must simply get started! We tried several curriculums for elementary school, and the truth is, we loved something about every one of them. I'll share some of the curriculums we used, but if this overwhelms you right now, you can just skim over this section. Come back to it once you've begun your own curriculum search, and it will make a lot more sense.

When I first started homeschooling my boys, Josiah was in second grade and Jonah was in kindergarten. Luke went to preschool that year. I decided to start with an all-in-one box curriculum by Sonlight, which was designed to be used for up to two to three grade levels *together* (a great feature if you have two kids close in age). Sonlight is a literature-based curriculum, with most of the topics covered through reading great stories. And boy, do they have great stories! (I still order reader books off Sonlight's online list because I really trust them to be good.)

I loved doing school with both boys at once, and I will forever treasure those days. The boys did math and language separately, and they had their own reader books as well. But I have wonderful memories of spending the bulk of our school days reading stories about world history, then getting out a huge dry-erase map that came with the curriculum and locating and drawing on the areas we learned about. We'd play music (I recall it was a cassette tape, *thankyouverymuch*) to memorize countries and capitals. (Josiah memorized all the countries in Africa that year. I bet he can still sing them today!)

The only problem I had with this curriculum—and it was a pretty serious issue—was that I discovered that I get extremely sleepy when I read out loud. Like, bad (insert laugh/cry emoji). I am convinced that this tendency is genetic, because my dad says he has always had the same issue. This meant that sadly, as much as I loved the books I was reading aloud to my boys, I could hardly keep my eyes open after just a few pages. I laugh now, but if you've ever experienced the torture of trying to keep your eyes open when you're really, really tired, you know this was not funny at the time.

Somehow we stuck with Sonlight for two full years (I drank a lot of coffee back then and learned to stand up while reading aloud), but then we began to dabble in other curriculums. By that time, I was more familiar with homeschooling and had talked to other homeschool moms and attended homeschool conferences. I felt ready to branch out and piece together my own combination of curriculums, based on my sons' learning styles and what worked best for me.

We ended up using some Abeka curriculum along with Sonlight readers, as well as Math-U-See and Teaching Textbooks for math. I list a few more excellent elementary curriculums in the next section on upper elementary age, and I also include a list of favorite elementary curriculums in the resource section. There are many to choose from, and I honestly did not *dislike* anything we tried.

Whether you use an all-in-one curriculum or choose to piece together your own, consider which subjects you feel are important for laying a groundwork for higher learning later. (Again, your child really doesn't need a lot of academics in these early years.) I also encourage you to leave plenty of hours of the day open for kids to continue to play freely and to explore their developing interests and passions, which is likely to become one of the best parts of homeschooling.

## Subjects to Cover in Early Elementary School

### Reading

Reading aloud is a wonderful perk of homeschooling the elementary years. Reading aloud has countless learning benefits. It helps children to develop greater vocabulary and learn to process information. It inspires kids through stories, introduces them to new ideas and concepts, and presents elements of language, like rhyming and alliteration, in a gentle and natural way. Beyond the academic benefits, reading aloud can be a bonding experience. Keep reading aloud every day if possible. If you are like me and struggle to stay awake, try to read aloud during the time of day when you are most alert and awake.

Each of my boys recalls different favorite read-aloud books, including many from the Heroes Then and Now Series (especially *George Müller* and *Gladys Aylward*, both by Janet and Geoff Benge), *My Father's Dragon* by Ruth Stiles Gannett, *Dolphin Adventure* and *Dolphin Treasure* by Wayne Grover, *Red Sails to Capri* by Ann Weil, *Bud, Not Buddy* by Christopher Paul Curtis, *Carry On, Mr. Bowditch* by Jean Lee Latham, and *Hinds Feet on High Places* by Hannah Hurnard, among so many others. (I've included a link to a list of our family's favorite books in the resource section.)

I also love that reading aloud opens up conversations about important, or even awkward, topics that we may want to have with our kids but aren't sure how to begin. Reading good books together has led to many conversations with my boys about sickness and death, race, other cultures, different religions and philosophies, and other weighty topics.

Most kids will also begin reading independently during their elementary years. Keep in mind that every child will learn to read at a different pace, and many tools are available to support your child in that process. Interestingly, after my initial worry that I wouldn't be able to teach my kids to read, the process ended up being quite natural. We found phonics programs to be helpful and made books a fun and special part of the boys' school days.

Some kids are eager to sound out words; others find patterns and learn to read more like solving a puzzle. Don't stress about the process; just enjoy supporting each student individually. Of course, if you hit major roadblocks or if it seems like your child is struggling beyond what is normal, you can find helpful resources online. Talk to your pediatrician if you have any medical or developmental concerns.

## Math

The early elementary years are important for helping kids build a foundation for understanding math concepts. You don't want to spend too much time on math at this age, or your child is likely to hate it, but ten to fifteen minutes a day should help your child develop basic math skills and give them the confidence and desire to want to learn more.

Math can be a frustrating subject to teach, and I regret memories of raising my voice and pounding my pointer finger on a math problem, as if that might open the channels of understanding. My impatience only exasperated my sons and made me feel like a jerk. Try to relax and trust that with consistency and short lessons, simple addition and subtraction will eventually begin to click. Also, do not think for a minute that math challenges in the younger years are a foreshadowing of the future. Math concepts build on one another, and sometimes the early stuff is the hardest. Jonah, who I remember struggled most with math in the early years, is now a mathematical genius. In fact, his summer job last year was working for a homeschool curriculum publisher as an editor for their Calculus 2 curriculum.

### Language (aka "Grammar")

Though some would advise holding off on grammar in early elementary school, I think most kids are ready to begin a basic language arts curriculum at this point. Many of these curriculums incorporate grammar, phonics, spelling, and reading into the lessons. As with math, you want to give kids only short lessons to begin with and consider it an introduction to what they'll really dive into later. Don't stress if they don't grasp all the concepts right away. In fact, if they hate it, put it away and try again in six months. (Yes, you can do that!)

### Handwriting

Copy work, which is simply copying lines of writing (in print or cursive), builds a great foundation for kids' future writing skills. In kindergarten and first grade, you'll want to keep writing lessons short and fun, and often kids will enjoy tracing over letters and numbers and eventually copying full sentences. There are a lot of great copy work resources available, and I love to use Bible verses as copy work to reinforce Scripture the kids are learning while also having them practice their handwriting. Be sure to display their work—it will make them feel proud of themselves.

### To Cursive or Not to Cursive?

Fewer and fewer kids are learning cursive handwriting today, and I will not tell you whether or not you ought to teach it. I required all my boys to learn cursive, though my husband challenged me on this decision. He suggested it would be more beneficial for the boys to learn to type on a keyboard, and he was probably right (I waited longer than I should have for that), but there's no reason why kids can't learn both. The way I see it, being able to handwrite a note in cursive might just set our kids apart one day. It's also a great way to develop fine motor skills and hand-eye coordination.

### Science, History, Geography, and More

Homeschooling topics like science, history, and geography is debatable in the early years. As I have previously confessed, I tend to find security in checking boxes and feeling like I've covered anything my kids would have learned in a traditional school. (This is probably a weakness of mine, so don't necessarily follow my lead.) I have always been drawn to all-in-one curriculums, which typically include at least simple lessons for all the main subjects for elementary-age kids.

Looking back, I probably pushed more than I needed to on some subjects during those early elementary years. Does Levi remember anything he learned in second-grade science? I doubt it. Yet I do wonder if my boys had an easier time transitioning to the more rigorous courses of the middle and high school years because they'd already built a foundation in each subject. Most seasoned homeschool parents would suggest that if your kids enjoy it, do it. If they don't, then wait.

### Art, Music, and Extracurriculars

Between kindergarten and third grade is a great time to introduce your kids to all kinds of art and music. They don't need formal classes as much as to have fun with paper and paints, glue, musical instruments, and anything else you can offer them. Early elementary kids are often ready for simple gymnastics or dance classes, swimming, and team sports. These are not "school" formally, but a lot of learning goes on in every new activity.

A word of caution: If you love all the extracurriculars, great. But do be careful—you don't want to overbook your youngster to the point that they lose the homeschooling benefit of having an abundance of downtime to play and use their imaginations. I encourage a healthy balance of some structured activities and plenty of relaxed time at home. Unstructured play will continue to be one of the most important parts of your child's day for many years to come.

# Upper Elementary Years (Grades 4-6)

*(Note: I'm including sixth grade in both upper elementary and middle school because it can land in either, and depending on preference/maturity level, homeschooling families can put their sixth grader in either category.)*

The second half of a child's elementary years is exceedingly special. Children are growing and changing a lot, and homeschool parents get to enjoy the last years of true "childhood" before kids hit the middle school and high school years.

The good news is that your fourth through sixth grader is likely to have developed more independence in their learning. Most of the time, they can read independently, and some of the time they even enjoy school. These are years to keep training your child, and you do need to stay involved in their school day, but you can also begin to pass more responsibility on to them.

Your child's developing personality will be emerging more during these years as well, so this is a good time to be a student of your student. Consider their learning style, their love language, and their general personality type. Take their birth order into account, along with other factors that might impact their days. Our first three sons transitioned well to more independent schooling, but our fourth son seemed to need (ahem, want) us by his side for as much of his school day as possible (and he still does). This initially frustrated me until my husband pointed out that this made sense according to his personality type. Levi thrives when working with people. He does not like to be alone. Recognizing his unique personality helped me to realize that I have a great opportunity to work on independence with him.

## Curriculum and Subjects to Cover

I think that using an official curriculum in these years is very helpful. While some families can find free resources online and use good books and other tools to teach their kids, grades four through six are academically foundational to the rest of your child's education, so this is an ideal time to consider investing in what will be most helpful to your child. My older boys transitioned from Sonlight to a variety of curriculums in the later homeschool years. I'll cover some of what we have used by subject, and you can find a more detailed overview of curriculums in the resource section at the end of the book.

### Reading and Language Arts

By fourth grade, most kids can read independently, and this is the perfect time to continue to provide them with great books so they develop a love for reading. Kids' reading levels vary a lot at this age, and it is not unusual for some kids to struggle with reading and put up a fight over it. *Boys especially.* Some of my sons put up a fight over reading assignments, but I have tried to stay firm, requiring a minimum amount of reading each school day. Finding book on topics that interest your kids is key, so give your family grace to figure this out. One of my sons loved science fiction novels, and another was drawn to true stories. Levi enjoys graphic novels (what we used to call comic books), and he will devour a good survival story. My personal preference is to have kids read old, classic, and award-winning novels over new, trending books. I appreciate the focus on character and values and many of the old fashioned, character-rich stories. While some newer stories are good and many are entertaining, I still lean toward those that have stood the test of time.

My friend Andrew Pudewa of the Institute for Excellence in Writing suggests a creative way to entice kids to want to read: Find a great books to read aloud to your child, and then when you hit an exciting part of the story, say, "Sorry, but we 'have to' put the book down now to go do something else." If you leave the book marked on the page where you left off and walk away, your child is likely to pick it up and keep reading. Recently I did this at bedtime with Levi, and he ended up finishing the book that night. That was fun!

### Math

Math can be super fun or super stressful for kids in upper elementary. Thankfully, there are great curriculums that help you homeschool this subject. I have enjoyed doing math with my boys (most of the time), but if you struggle with math, there are some great video curriculums available. Teaching Textbooks was one they enjoyed during this season (and I hear from a lot of other homeschoolers who love it), as well as Math-U-See, which uses hands-on manipulatives for help in understanding place value and other concepts. Some of my boys used Abeka videos for math as well, which were thorough but required a longer attention span.

I have found that most math curriculums have unreasonably long assignments, so this is a good example of a time to fully embrace your role as a homeschool parent. Remember, you don't have to do every problem! I almost always allowed Levi to do only odd or even problems in his Saxon Math 7/6 book this year. And those still weren't short lessons. I am a stickler for math because I know how helpful it is as kids get older. (Think SAT and ACT scores.) But I don't think an upper elementary student needs to spend a full hour on math each day. It might be wise to figure out how much time your child is able to spend on math before they fizzle out, and then set a timer for that. I'm all for teaching kids to persevere and do hard things, but as homeschool parents, we also need wisdom to know when we're not being reasonable.

### History and Science

Some homeschool experts would suggest that when it comes to history and science, you continue to stick with interest-based learning in the upper elementary years, and if you feel good about that philosophy, then you are probably safe to do that. For example, perhaps you read a story about an explorer that sparks your child's interest. This can lead to reading more stories or getting out a map or doing an art project from that story. This happens a lot for Levi—after learning a little bit about a place or topic, he will often want to explore more on Google Earth, and soon he is jotting down notes in a notebook and printing pictures of places he hopes to visit one day. (All of this while not realizing he is actually learning.) However, I have used a basic science, history, and/or geography curriculum for all my boys in their upper elementary years, which helps me feel like we've covered the basics and they're better prepared for higher level classes later.

### Writing

A good language arts program will introduce kids to writing, but being a writer myself, I have loved giving my boys a solid introduction to writing in the upper elementary years. My boys all started using IEW (Institute for Excellence in Writing) in fourth grade, and later they all agreed it was an excellent foundation for future writing (specifically for college entrance essays). Levi resisted seriously at first, but just last week he told me IEW was his favorite class.

Typically, girls enjoy writing more than boys at this age, but a good curriculum will give you tools to inspire even the most hesitant boy writer. Incorporating interesting animals, explosions, or anything with action is helpful—a tip I learned from Mr. Pudewa.

## What Your Elementary Child Needs Most

Most homeschooling families I know look back on the elementary years with fond memories. While giving your kids a good education is important, these years are important for helping them grow in their identity as God's children—loved and secure. This is the time to give your children a strong family unit that will be there for them for all their years. This is the time to give them healthy food, plenty of sleep (oh, how they grow!), and the chance to keep being children in the most wholesome environment possible. I highly recommend keeping screen time (outside of school use) to a minimum. (Find more encouragement for managing screen time in my bonus chapter "Practical Help for Real Homeschool Challenges.") Get those elementary kids moving their bodies, creating, exploring, imagining . . . making music and muffins and watercolor masterpieces.

> While giving your kids a good education is important, these years are important for helping them grow in their identity as God's children—loved and secure.

The foundation you build in these years will prepare your children for all that is ahead—and it's a lot. You will never regret these very special years with your elementary children! For every challenge or frustration you encounter, you will find at least as many moments of wonder, exploration, and joy. There is no doubt that these are days you'll replay in your mind a thousand times later. You'll never regret making them the most enjoyable, memorable years possible.

## TAKE-HOME THOUGHT

Homeschooling in the elementary years gives you a chance to build an amazing foundation of learning, faith, and family bonds.

## REFLECTION QUESTION

What is one thing you want your elementary age child to take with them into the next season, and how might you pour into that now?

CHAPTER 7

# AWESOME AND AWKWARD

## Homeschooling Middle School

As I write this chapter, I am wrapping up Levi's seventh-grade year, and no doubt I have #allthemomfeels. One of the benefits of homeschooling my fourth and final child is that I have greater perspective this time. I am cherishing these days with appreciation and nostalgia. Even if middle school is still hard.

The truth is, I hardly remember my firstborn's seventh-grade year (understandably—I was busy with a fifth grader and a third grader, as well as a toddler). I have vague memories of all of the big brothers at this age, but now I have the focus and time to be fully present as my final boy forges his way through the wonderful, awkward, hilarious, emotional, transformative season of middle school.

Middle school has always been one of my favorite seasons (except when I was in it!). When Dave and I lived in Oregon, before we had kids, I taught middle school and high school. Dave and I also worked in youth ministry, so we spent a lot of time with this age group. It always fascinated me to see these kids transition, seemingly right in front of my eyes, from gangly tweens to full-grown teenagers.

In one of my most-read blog posts, "What a Middle School Boy Needs Most from His Parents," I wrote,

> The tricky thing with middle school boys is that there is a huge range of developmental and maturity level among them. You may have a sixth grader who is developmentally still like a fourth grader. On the other hand, you may have an eighth grader who looks and sounds like a seventeen-year-old. Things are happening at an inconsistent rate, wildly varying from one young body to the next.
>
> And perhaps your greatest job during these years is to study that boy and determine just where he is in that range. You, the parent, will know the very best where your son is developmentally and maturity-wise, and you must parent him accordingly. Not according to a number (grade or age). Not according to what his friends are doing. According to what is the very best thing for your son, in the stage he is currently in.
>
> Hitting the middle school years is like getting to halftime of an important game: You may be ahead now, but the game's not over. Towel off, get a big drink of water, and then gear up for the second half. You want to finish strong.[1]

If you have the chance to homeschool a middle schooler, I highly recommend you do it. In fact, if you had to choose only one stage to homeschool, I'd almost always vote for middle school.

## What Middle Schoolers Are Dealing With

Before we dive into the nitty-gritty of academics in sixth through eighth grade, I think it is wise to talk a little bit about the nuances of a middle schooler's human experience. This should help us to be a bit more understanding and compassionate with our kids, and it also might give you the motivation you need to commit to homeschooling.

I don't mean to paint a scary picture of the middle school years, but I think it is wise to consider all the changes taking place and why these years can be especially challenging.

## Puberty

Puberty, which generally begins between the age of ten and twelve (earlier for girls than boys, typically) is an unavoidable part of the middle school years. Long before you see physical changes in your child, you may notice other signs of increased hormones— from serious sleepiness to sporadic hyperactivity, from hysterical laughter to uncontrollable tears. If there is one word to summarize puberty, it is *change*. And change is happening in every area of your middle schooler's life.

## Brain Development

Besides the first three years of life, recent research has found that the next great growth spurt in the human brain occurs between the ages of eleven and fourteen. Middle school kids are able to think more complexly than they did previously and begin to form their own ideas and opinions. Yet despite their developing brains, the pre-frontal cortex—the primary decision-making part of the brain—is far from fully developed. Middle school kids still need a lot of supervision, though they often like to believe they do not. This can make parenting—and homeschooling—middle schoolers a challenge.[2]

## Physical Development

Middle schoolers' bodies are typically smack-dab in the middle of some crazy growth spurts. If your eleven- to fourteen-year-old hasn't grown a few inches this year, they are probably about to. And their growth is rarely graceful; instead, they often grow in an unco-ordinated rhythm—legs and arms first, body next, giving them the awkward reputation middle schoolers are famous for.

During this time, kids' genitals are also changing, and pubic hair is developing. Girls develop breasts and begin their menstrual cycle. Kids will become more curious about their sexuality and have a lot of questions. Curiosity about sexuality is typically awkward, and unless an intentional parent is an actively available resource, middle schoolers will often turn to their peers or to the internet to figure things out. It is not a coincidence that most boys see pornography for the first time between ages nine and twelve. Sadly, by high school, many boys are well on their way to pornography addiction.

## Emotional Development

Perhaps one of the most challenging parts of this stage of adolescence is the emotional roller coaster that is often associated with it. As their brains and bodies are experiencing explosive growth and their self-consciousness peaks, middle schoolers are also facing more rigorous classes and increased pressure in sports and other activities. All of this is happening just as new hormones are coursing through their bodies, wreaking havoc on their emotions. I don't think it's an exaggeration to say, it's a lot!

## Social Development

During the middle school years, kids become more conscious of their peers and more aware of their own identities. They want to fit in and will sometimes go to great lengths to do so. Without some guidance in handling these new urges, middle schoolers often find themselves succumbing to peer pressure and making dangerous choices.

Middle school kids left without supervision are likely to be curious and want to explore—in the neighborhood and on the internet—as well as embrace questionable relationships, illegal substances, alternative identities, and so many other risky things. Many young adults with serious life regrets recall middle school insecurity as the catalyst for their first serious, bad choices.

### Spiritual Development

By middle school, kids often are asking more questions about the faith their parents have raised them with. Depending on how this is handled by their parents and others around them, a middle schooler might solidify their faith and develop a true, personal relationship with God, or they might begin a departure from what their parents taught them growing up.

Each of my boys wrestled with worldview concepts during middle school, bringing up good questions about heaven and hell, God's sovereignty, and Christ's assurance of salvation. Dave and I found this to be a great opportunity to open God's Word together and help them discover answers to their questions. However, if those questions are left unanswered, or if kids see hypocrisy in their parents or bad examples of Christianity in their church community, they are prone to search elsewhere for meaning and purpose.

## So . . . What Do Middle Schoolers Need Most?

With all the changes going on during the middle school years, it is clear why the environment your child spends time in is so important.

Middle schoolers need a safe place where they can process emotions, ask questions, and simply be themselves—even if they aren't so sure of who they are yet.

Middle schoolers need parents to set boundaries and offer expanding freedoms as they earn their parents' trust.

Middle schoolers need adults who listen and engage with them on a deeper level, affirming their growing maturity.

Middle schoolers need access to helpful resources and positive influences outside of Mom and Dad.

Middle schoolers need to do some hard, physical labor—yard work and household chores, as well as other outside jobs they're capable of doing.

Middle schoolers need a lot of sleep, healthy and nourishing food, and plenty of exercise.

Middle schoolers need to be assured that their emotions are normal, while being coached on how to regulate them. They need to be reminded that they (and their feelings) are not the center of the universe, and they also need to be reminded to consider other peoples' feelings.

> Middle schoolers need a safe place where they can process emotions, ask questions, and simply be themselves—even if they aren't so sure of who they are yet.

Socially, middle schoolers need to find healthy, safe places where they can spend time with friends. A strong church youth program can be a great place to make friends (but that's not a guarantee—more on that at the end of this chapter). Sports teams or other extracurricular activities often provide a great social environment for middle schoolers, as these groups generally include many kids who come from supportive, involved families.

While friendships are important in middle school, this is a season in which friendships can get tricky, which is another reason they need the support of understanding parents. My boys, and many other young adults I have talked to, found that during middle school many of their childhood friends pulled away from their faith and began to hang out with a crowd of kids who were getting into trouble.

My boys were torn between trying to keep established friendships (while hoping they could be a good influence on their friends) or not having many friends. While we prayed for the friends our sons were formerly close to and encouraged them to make new friends, my husband and I set some boundaries on their time with their former friends. (We did not allow them to hang out with these friends when trusted adults were not around, and invited the kids to our home if they wanted to hang out.)

Since we lived in a small community without a lot of social options, some of these hard choices led to lonely seasons for our kids. However, it was during this season that they developed many of their interests and passions—from guitar and photography to surfing, skating, and computer coding. They grew in their friendship with God, and they became more content spending time at home with their family. (We were actually way cooler than they realized!) And over time, they developed solid friendships with some of the youth group kids and leaders they continued to spend time with.

Looking back, my boys are grateful we said no to their requests to hang out with certain kids, because they know they were spared some vulnerable situations, and they realize how much they gained, even in the lonely season.

Most of all, middle schoolers need to be assured that the God who made them loves them and has answers for their toughest questions—including, and maybe especially those related to, identity. Because there is no doubt: identity formation is a big part of the middle school years. And we have a great opportunity to teach our kids what the Bible says about them—being made in the image of God and having great worth apart from their performance or popularity. These messages of truth can make a massive difference in a kid's middle school experience.

We must warn our children that the world will offer them all kinds of lies; they'll be told that truth is relative, that the Bible is irrelevant, and that their feelings are the most important thing. But only the God who made them and loves them more than anyone else (including even their parents) can be trusted to assign them purpose and value. These are big and difficult topics, but oh, what a gift is a parent who is willing to speak these truths boldly and confidently, for our kids are listening, even when they're pretending they're not.

It's hard to imagine a better place for a middle schooler to experience all these things than their own home, under the supervision of the people who love them deeply and are most invested in their future. Indeed, homeschooling in middle school is a really, really good idea.

Now that we've covered the nuances of a middle schoolers' experience (it's a lot, right?), let's see how all of that can play out in a homeschool environment.

### More Independent Learning

The good news is, your middle schooler should be gaining some independence in their schoolwork, especially if they have been homeschooling for some time. You shouldn't expect your child to do their work without *any* supervision, but they should take on more responsibility every year.

This is a great age to talk to your kids about developing strong study habits. Help them find the important parts in a textbook to highlight or take notes on. Coach them in reviewing material before a quiz or test, and have fun making a game of oral quizzes or memorization challenges. I have been working with Levi on planning out his week on a calendar, anticipating assignments and tests and strategizing for upcoming holidays or breaks. I love seeing him take more ownership of his schedule, and while he still needs a few reminders, I am seeing the potential for a self-directed learner down the road.

## Keeping Records

You will want to keep up on your state's legal requirements, but you usually don't have to create a formal transcript for middle school. I do recommend, however, that you use this as a time to practice for high school, when you *will* need to create a transcript. You might start using an official homeschool record book or use any format that works for you to keep track of how many hours your child spends on classes a week and what their grades are by semester. If you haven't already, I would also suggest practicing for and taking standardized tests during middle school. (Some states require standardized tests in certain grades, so keep an eye on the HSLDA/legal webpage.) Standardized tests can be helpful to track how your child is progressing academically and to find any weak points you might need to focus on in the upcoming year. This is completely up to you as a family, and I understand that not everyone likes tests, but I do think it's a good idea to practice. (We'll talk more about standardized testing in chapter 9.)

## Subjects and Curriculum

The middle school years continue to be a time of freedom to explore curriculums for various subjects. My goal has always been to find the best curriculum fit for my boys before high school starts because I want to avoiding switching things around too much during the high school years. While some kids find a curriculum that works for all their subjects, often by middle school you will find a few different curriculums that work best for various subjects. For us, that looked like the Abeka online videos and books for most of the humanities (grammar, literature, and history) and the DIVE and Shormann curriculum for science and math.

In middle school, your student should cover the core subjects of math, grammar, reading, and writing. History, science, and health are optional, and some homeschool parents think it's not important to officially begin them, but I feel best getting a middle schooler's feet wet in these topics before they begin high school.

By sixth or seventh grade, your child will likely be gravitating toward certain subjects. That is a good indicator of where their interests lie, but try not to let that deter you from including the less-liked subjects in their school day. Sometimes kids think they don't like a subject, but it's only because they have not yet mastered it. Levi thought he didn't like math, but after pushing through some frustrating lessons, complete with a lot of tears and "I hate math!" comments, concepts began to click for him. Some light bulbs came on, and soon he realized he was pretty good at math after all. Now he has more frequent moments of taking pride in his work—whether math or writing or science—which may be just as rewarding for me as it is for him.

### Electives

Just like in the elementary years, one of the biggest benefits of homeschooling middle school is the chance to explore all the subjects that don't fall under the category of "core curriculum." Hopefully by now your child has discovered a few of their passions and interests, and this is the time to let them dive in deeper. For those kids who are new to homeschooling, this is the perfect time to explore all that is available to them. In particular, the more time your child spends outdoors, the better, and these are great years to offer them a lot of opportunities to move their body. These are also crucial years to set firm rhythms and routines for screen time. Even if you developed some less-than-ideal screen habits in the earlier years, you can teach that part of the responsibility of being in middle school is learning time management. And there are too many important things to do in a day (from work to school to sports to other activities) to waste time looking at a screen. Typically, tweens and young teens have more than a little energy to burn, so encourage them to get active with organized sports, biking, running, swimming, skateboarding, or whatever they can find.

Middle school is also a great time for kids to invest time and effort in learning a musical instrument, exploring various types of art, and studying a foreign language. My oldest son, Josiah, who studied data analytics in college and now works in the computer industry, recommends that all middle schoolers begin to learn computer coding. Encourage kids to delve into topics they find interesting through books or the internet (with filters in place and in observable locations). This is a wonderful age for field trips, and middle schoolers are often great travel companions as you explore museums, galleries, zoos, or other attractions. Your student might bring along a notebook or journal to take notes for a follow-up report or journal entry after an outing. You'll find a list of possible electives in the resource section.

### Service

If you haven't started this already, middle school is a great time to get your child involved in service projects. They can be organized, like working at a church-run food bank, or spontaneous, like helping make a meal for a family who just had a baby or visiting the elderly in a nursing home. Like my homeschooling friend Tiffany says, "We are called to love our neighbors, and what better way for a child to learn to do that than to practically love and serve those in their life? I want my kids to grow up with service as a normal rhythm of life."

With a little research, you'll find many opportunities throughout the week to allow your child to serve others and, in turn, develop more compassion and perspective. Middle school kids tend to be self-absorbed, and serving others can help remedy that.

## Bible Curriculum and Personal Faith Development

If you use a Christian curriculum, it is likely to include a daily Bible lesson. You can also find a good variety of Bible curriculums online. My boys have almost always used an Abeka Bible curriculum, which is thorough—and not short. My oldest sons didn't seem to mind, but Levi seems to have a shorter attention span, so this curriculum has been more of a challenge for him. Since Levi does daily devotions (more on that in a moment) instead of an actual Bible curriculum, we used the Foundation Worldview curriculum in his seventh-grade year. This has been a great option for him that has led to many good conversations. In future years, I plan to use a true Bible curriculum with him, as my three older boys have all told me they are grateful for all they learned in these classes and highly recommend I don't give up on having Levi use one (thanks, boys).

Since middle schoolers are developing their own independent thoughts and opinions, they are also likely to be thinking more critically through matters of faith. They might have more questions than they did previously, and depending on their personalities and the relationships parents have established with them, they may or may not voice these questions or doubts out loud. Peers can influence this process greatly, for better or for worse. Church youth programs are sometimes a blessing at this age, but not always. Some youth programs actually end up being a gathering place for kids looking for trouble. I recommend that parents check out a youth group, even sticking around on the sidelines, if possible, a time or two to observe how it's run and to notice any areas of concern before leaving kids there alone. In fact, many youth groups welcome parent volunteers, so that might be a good option as well. Once again, this is a time to be a student of your student, prayerfully considering the best environment to encourage and nurture a strong faith in them.

By the time they reached middle school, I had encouraged my boys to begin doing daily devotions (Bible reading, prayer, and sometimes a devotional book) independently. Devotional books are available, as well as online devotions through the YouVersion Bible app or other helpful sites like the Fellowship of Christian Athletes online devotional. I also encouraged my middle schoolers to begin a prayer and Bible journaling habit. At this age, they were often resistant to the idea ("more writing?!"), but I only asked them to write a Bible verse, a short prayer, or even a line about what they were learning about God in it most days. I think prayer journaling is a great discipline, so I tried to help my kids start it young. By the time my older boys were in later high school, they independently used a prayer journal quite consistently. (Find a link to a printable prayer and Bible journaling template in the resource section.)

## Good News

Most of us think back to our middle school years with a cringe and perhaps some gratitude that they are far behind us. Without a doubt, our kids' middle school years will be filled with change and likely some challenges too. Yet here is some good news I can tell you about homeschooling middle school: my older three boys have never communicated negative memories of their middle school experience. They might remember pimples, braces, and some awkward phases, but they don't talk about disliking their middle school experience overall. I think this is because they transitioned from child to tween to teen in a natural, secure environment. They spent much of their time at home. They were not confronted daily with

> What a difference you can make in your middle schooler's life with your steady presence, unconditional love, and a willingness to laugh.

social pressures or comparisons. They had freedom to be goofy or happy or somewhere in between while working through daily routines of school, play, chores, and all the rest. And they had Mom and Dad coaching, disciplining, and cheering them on the entire way. There are not many greater gifts you can give than that of homeschooling your middle schooler. What a difference you can make in your middle schooler's life with your steady presence, unconditional love, and a willingness to laugh—because middle schoolers can be very, very funny!

## TAKE-HOME THOUGHT

Middle school is one of the most complicated and challenging seasons in a child's life, and it may be the most important time to give them the gift of homeschooling.

## REFLECTION QUESTION

What are the greatest challenges facing your middle schooler, and how might you help them through this stage of their life in the context of a homeschooling experience?

## CHAPTER 8

# INDEPENDENT AND INSPIRED

## Homeschooling High School

If the thought of homeschooling high school makes your blood pressure rise, you are not alone. Most parents I talk to experience something between mild anxiety and all-out panic as they imagine homeschooling high schoolers. (Spoiler alert: It's not that scary—or difficult!)

I remember all the questions looming over me well before we hit the high school years:

> *Do I have what it takes to give my kids a high school education?*
> *Will I forget something and completely blow my kids' future opportunities?*
> *Will my kids figure out how little I actually know?*
> *Am I supposed to still remember algebra, ancient history, and the periodic table?*

Surely, we tell ourselves, someone else could educate them better than we can.

I'll never forget a conversation I had with a friend the year before my oldest son started high school. She lived in Portland, Oregon, and her kids went to a newly established classical Christian school. They were a few years ahead of mine, and the whole family was thrilled with their school experience.

I mentioned to my friend that Josiah seemed to be drawn mostly to science and math thus far, and with enthusiasm in her voice, she threw out an idea: "You should send Josiah over to live with us next year! Our school just built a multimillion-dollar science wing that he would thrive in."

Anxiety enveloped me as I reflected on Josiah's homeschool science curriculum, which thus far had consisted of reading a textbook and watching a teacher perform experiments on a video. I felt lame realizing I hadn't so much as ordered the basic equipment to allow my son to do the experiments at home. As my friend finished detailing all the bells and whistles of her kids' super-awesome school, insecurity and fear moved front and center in my mind. I began to doubt everything about my silly attempt to homeschool Josiah—as if I could ever actually compete with a "real" school.

Those thoughts plagued me for a few solid minutes (or perhaps a week), but after praying and having some good conversations with my husband, I snapped out of it. Thankfully, by this point I had homeschooled long enough to have some confidence in what we were giving our son. And though our family's homeschool setup wasn't anything close to a science wing that cost seven figures to construct, we *were* giving him a lot more. While it wouldn't hurt to up my game and at least order some proper science equipment, I recommitted to saying no to comparison or insecurity.

The truth is, I never did get fancy science equipment for Josiah—or for any of my sons. We did, however, find an online high school science and math curriculum that they loved with a teacher they respected. Josiah continued to thrive in these classes and was able to take courses through AP calculus and physics. All while continuing to homeschool. Later he went on to college, where he took rigorous science classes—complete with real labs. No one realized he'd never done an actual lab before, and he graduated with nearly all As.

Every child's experience will be different, of course, but I hope this story gives you a little extra confidence that you can give your child a great high school experience, even with a simple homeschool education (and no lab equipment).

(By the way, I ordered an eighth-grade science experiment kit for Levi shortly after writing this chapter. Thank you for the accountability check!)

## Transitioning into High School

In chapter 7, we talked about the developmental changes to expect during middle school, and many of these changes will continue into high school. The good news is, homeschooling offers kids a stable and secure environment in which they can grow and change and mature. Remembering my own transition from middle school to high school and all the new challenges and pressures that came with it, I appreciate knowing that homeschooling allows us to avoid many of the unnecessary challenges during this stage.

### Get Prepared

Our kids are not the only ones experiencing change; as we homeschool and parent our growing kids, we will be growing and changing too. We'll be finding our footing and adjusting to new roles and relationships with our kids. We'll be needed in different ways, and our role will be shifting to more that of "coach" and "mentor." Your kids still need you, along with boundaries, discipline, and order. But they also need to develop more independence. They

> Your kids still need you, along with boundaries, discipline, and order. But they also need to develop more independence.

need to make choices and experience consequences in school and in all areas of life. And you need to let them.

A homeschooled high schooler will have many great opportunities to venture into independence, and parents who support them enthusiastically will be a great blessing.

Remember to be kind to your high schooler and to yourself as your whole family learns how to navigate this new season. That said, prepare yourself for certain situations, and don't be surprised if . . .

**Sometimes kids aren't excited about homeschooling.** Be aware that kids who were previously content to homeschool might reach ninth or tenth grade and ask to go to a conventional school. This might be due to their growing independence, or they might be concerned that they are missing out on something, or they might have some other reason for their interest.

It is always important to listen to your kids and to consider their thoughts and feelings because there might be a valid reason to consider a change. But I encourage you to get back to the core reasons your family chose to homeschool and not to give up on homeschooling too quickly.

As I mentioned earlier, when Jonah began to ask to go to public high school, I genuinely explored the option of sending him. But our Hawaii laws would have required him to begin as a ninth grader, even though he'd already completed his freshman year. Repeating ninth grade was not a reasonable option for my then sixteen-year-old son, so this was disappointing at the time. However, looking back, we are all so glad. Years later, Jonah voiced his gratitude for being "stuck" as a homeschooler. He ended up having a great high school experience—homeschooling all the way through—and has no regrets now.

**Kids face some lonely seasons.** Like the middle school years, the high school years can be lonely. I have shared my older boys' story of seeing a lot of their friends choose to walk away from faith during the early teen years. We had many conversations about whether or not they should continue to pursue those relationships or if it would be better to step away. None of it was easy. We all want our kids to have good friends, and seeing them lonely can be hard. But in our family's case, there was a season when the boys mostly hung out with us, other than when they did sports or were at youth group. This was a time when they developed skills and grew in their walk with God. By the end of high school, they had settled into some new friendships with kids from youth group, and then in college they found many more friends who shared their faith and their interests. Lonely seasons can be hard, but it is better for a child to be lonely than to be brought down by friends who are making bad choices.

## Academic Considerations

Homeschooling in the high school years will require some planning and recordkeeping on your part. It's not nearly as bad as most people imagine, however, so I do hope this chapter and the next will provide you with some assurance that you really can do this. For a deeper dive into any of the topics covered in this chapter, you will find all the links you need in the resource section at the end of the book.

As we talked about in chapter 4, you should always be familiar with the legal homeschooling requirements in your specific state. (The Homeschool Legal Defense Association [HSLDA] website offers everything you need to know for each state.) What you'll find is that, although *there may be legal requirements* for turning in progress reports and/or taking standardized tests at certain intervals during your students' school years, most states *do not have academic graduation requirements* for homeschoolers. Yes, you read that right! Very few states have academic requirements for homeschoolers to graduate.

If your child plans to go to college or trade school or another type of professional school after high school, there will be admission requirements for that (which we'll get to in a moment). But currently only a couple of states require specific courses or credits for your child to legally graduate from homeschooling high school. *You* get to decide what you will require for your child to graduate from high school.

This is great news, right?

For many of us, however, this news can leave us feeling a bit uneasy and insecure. *How do I decide which classes my high school child should take?* we wonder. Don't worry—there are some steps you can take to simplify your decision-making.

**1. If your child is planning to attend college (or you at least want to keep that door open, which I recommend), then you should find out what is required to get into the colleges they are interested in.** You can do that easily by visiting the websites of those specific schools. Every college has different admission requirements, so it is wise to research them online and search for their "general admissions" or "catalog" section. There you will find a list of how many credits of various subjects are required, along with any specific courses the admissions department wants to see on a college application. Visiting a variety of college websites to gather ideas is wise. Perhaps you can check out what a state college requires, as well as a private school and a community college.

If your child is not planning to attend college, you can follow the same process for any career path they are interested in. You can do a search online for requirements to become a plumber, an esthetician, a mechanic, and so on. Take your time doing this—it is truly interesting and helpful. (The next chapter will cover much more about the college preparatory, application, and admissions processes.)

**2. Find out what the graduation requirements are for public schools.** Yes, you read that right. This was a step that brought me a lot of assurance. I figured if I knew what it would take for my boys to graduate from a public school, my goal would be to give them that—plus a bit more.

This may sound silly, since part of why we are homeschooling is to avoid having to follow anything the public schools are doing, but discovering this information will help put your mind at ease. Why? Because by seeing what the public schools require, you can put to rest the fears that most of us have that we are missing something super important.

While you are checking out your local public school graduation requirements, you also might take a look at what other public schools across the country require. You'll see that there is a lot of variation across the nation. This, too, should offer you some assurance that there is not just one "right way" to homeschool your kids. In the resource section, I share a link to a full list of public schools with their graduation requirements.

I want to reiterate the importance of finding out your state's legal requirements for homeschooling (annual progress reports, standardized testing, and anything else), as well as any graduation requirements your state may require. This part is fully your responsibility as parents, and I suggest you *print out hard copies of all relevant documents*. I also suggest revisiting the HSLDA legal website (hslda.org/legal) to check on your state's laws at least once a year just in case things have changed.

## Mapping Out a High School Plan

With all this information researched and handy, you will next want to map out a high school plan *before your child is in high school*, if possible. If your child is younger, you might begin your high school plan in the eighth grade, because sometimes your child can tackle a class (or two or three) in eighth grade that you can count for high school credit. (This is a super-smart thing to do.) For example, Levi will take pre-algebra in eighth grade, which can be counted as a high school math credit.

You might use a homeschool planner or simply create your own plan online or on paper, charting out the basic coursework you would like your child to complete for each grade of high school. Again, your plan should include any specific requirements according to your child's specific post–high school plans, any specific state requirements you find at the HSLDA/legal website, and anything else you and your student might want to cover during high school.

There will be a lot of variations in the course plans for high schoolers in light of their interests and goals, but the following is one example of a high school plan for a (college-bound) high schooler:

(Be sure to check the resource section for links to much more detailed samples and advice.)

| | 8th | 9th | 10th | 11th | 12th |
|---|---|---|---|---|---|
| Math | Pre-Algebra | Algebra | Geometry | Pre-Calculus | Calculus* (or a year off math) |
| Science | Earth Science | Integrated Chemistry and Physics | Biology w/ lab | Chemistry w/ lab | Physics* w/ lab |
| History | | Geology/ State History | US History | World History | US Government |
| Language Arts | | Grammar 9 | Grammar 10/ Literature 10 | English Literature | Expository Writing/ British Literature* |
| Fine Arts Physical Ed. | | Music Weights/ Golf | Photography Running | Art Surfing/ Golf | Golf |

| Bible | | Christian Worldview | Old Testament Bible | New Testament Bible | Guidance/ Ministry |
|---|---|---|---|---|---|
| Foreign Language | | | Spanish 1 | Spanish 2 | Spanish 3 |
| Elective | | Computer Coding | Internship/ Elective | Internship/ Elective | Elective |

*examples of classes that might be good for advanced placement credits

You might write in general subject categories (like math) but wait until later to fill in the specific classes that will be taken (pre-algebra, algebra). You could just write in "elective" for each semester and then choose specific electives one year at a time. The good news is that you can tailor these plans to each student, depending on their goals and life circumstances. And of course you can adjust your plan as you progress. You'll find a variety of sample high school plans in the resource section, as well as plenty of other resources to help you with the planning process.

I didn't know where to begin planning for high school when Josiah was in middle school. I remember when he was in eighth grade, I met with a friend who was a few years ahead of me in home-schooling. Over cups of coffee, she helped me sketch out a four-year plan on a piece of notebook paper. The "plan" was as simple as a four-row chart listing the most important "core subjects" for ninth through twelfth grades, with a few blank spaces to fill in electives. Just seeing something written down on paper gave me confidence that I knew what needed to be done. Looking back, I don't think I had any idea how my friend decided what to put on that paper, and I didn't think to ask. (You don't know what you don't know.) If my friend had given me bad information or if I hadn't eventually checked our state laws, this could have been a terrible mistake, but fortunately it worked out for us.

As you'll read in the next chapter, we ended up working with a local group that created high school transcripts for my boys.

Unfortunately, the group we worked with no longer exists, so at this point I'm planning to do all of Levi's recordkeeping on my own.

## Recording Course Credits

Regardless of the legal requirements for homeschooling in your state, I recommend keeping records of all academics for your kid's high school years. I know some families don't believe this is necessary, but doing so gives me the security that if the laws changed or if for whatever reason I had to prove that we were educating our kids, I could. If your child is planning to go to college (or if you at least agree with me that it is wise to keep that door open), then this information is especially important.

To keep a record of your student's high school coursework, you will keep a record of class "credits." While a few states have very different ways of recording credits, most states record "credits" and "hours" as follows:

- A (1.00 unit) "credit" is given for a class that *lasts a full school year*—or two semesters (typically 150 to 180 "class hours" + more for labs or advanced placement classes). For example, a year of algebra or US history would equal a one-credit class, or approximately 170 hours.
- A (0.5 unit) "half credit" is given for a class that *lasts a half school year*—or one semester (approximately 75 to 90 "class hours").

Homeschool parents of high school students have the responsibility of planning and keeping track of how many credits their children complete during each year of high school. This process can be kept very simple: if you look at a school-year calendar and map out a simple schedule for your student, you'll see things clearly. For example, if you begin the school year in September and your child does a subject approximately an hour a day, five days a week (with holidays and a fall break off), they should be able to log 80 "class hours" in all their core subjects with plenty of room to spare by Christmas break.

From there, you have a lot of freedom. You might choose to start school earlier in the year (we typically begin school in August when Hawaii public schools begin), do school only four days a week, or pack more into your weeks and then take a big break for a vacation or the holidays. *You get to decide!* Just be sure to plan out your calendar so that your student completes the equivalent of a half or full credit per class (approximately 85 hours for a half credit and 170 hours for a full credit) for each class you are planning, and then *put that in writing*. Plan for around 5 to 7 credits per year for each year of high school.

Again, you can see what my boys did for high school—as well as what other families have done—in the resource section of the book. But also keep in mind, I filled in the specifics of my sons' classes as they went along. I didn't know Josiah would take geometry, algebra, pre-calculus, and calculus in high school. I only planned for four general math classes and figured out what he was ready for as he progressed. (He took pre-algebra in eighth grade, which was a great jump start for excelling in high school math.) Neither of my sons knew which electives they would take each year, but we wrote in "elective" for each semester of each year of high school. Later we decided on electives that included photography, guitar, video editing, and leadership for youth ministry.

## Planning the School Year

After choosing our curriculum each summer, I typically print out a blank yearlong calendar page and plan out our school year. I label the date we plan to begin and end, block off breaks and holidays, and then number the days according to the hours required for the school year. For example, each day we do math is a "one hour" math credit, whether my son gets it done in thirty minutes or an hour and a half (which we really try to avoid).

After creating these school-year calendars a couple of times, we've been able to repeat the same plan for upcoming school years. Once everything is penciled in, I never worry too much about whether we stay perfectly on schedule. I glance at it occasionally to see if we're close to the plan, and I love when we (rarely but sometimes) make it to the halfway point of our curriculum before Christmas break.

At the end of the school year, I write down the credit hours completed for that year. I also write a simple description of each subject with textbook or online resource used (title, publisher, and publishing date or website information). I stick it all in a file folder with my son's name and grade level for that year written across the front. And then I call it good. This is a sufficient recordkeeping strategy until it's time to create a high school transcript. (We'll get to that in the next chapter.)

Take a deep breath. This is all so doable!

I've included both a sample of our four-year plan (for the State of Hawaii) and an example of how I mapped out a school year in the resource section at the end of the book.

### Choosing Your Curriculum

Many wonderful high school curriculums are available, and the information in chapter 4 should help guide you in finding the best fit for your student. My goal was to find a curriculum or two (or three) that was a good fit for my boys to use for as much of high school as possible. The workload is heavier in high school, so a common curriculum offers some consistency, which I think is helpful. For example, they might start their day with an Abeka Bible video lecture, then go right into Abeka language arts, literature, and history (all with video lectures paired with textbooks and workbooks). Then, after a lunch break, they'd switch gears and do their Institute for Excellence in Writing class, followed by the Shormann and DIVE curriculums for math and science.

If you are starting homeschooling for the first time in high school, I recommend talking to other families and requesting samples from various homeschool curriculums to check out before you order anything. You may want to choose a curriculum with elements similar to the curriculum your student previously used in a classroom. If you switch from a traditional school setting to something extremely different, it might be too much change too quickly. (It also might be incredibly refreshing, but you know your child best.)

Depending on your child's post–high school goals, they may or may not need to pack heavy academics into each year. For example, most colleges require only three years of math in high school, so your student might enjoy skipping a year of math in the middle or looking forward to a senior year without math. But if your child is trying to get into a competitive college, hoping for an academic scholarship, or wanting to work in or study something math related after high school, then it is wise to take all four years of math. One of my sons got more serious about math after his sophomore year, so he decided to squeeze in a summer math class to allow himself to complete AP calculus before he graduated. There are many ways to fit classes in when you are homeschooling.

While high school will require more work than the previous years, hopefully that work is also interesting and exciting. Electives and extracurriculars, which we'll talk more about in chapter 10, will be an important part of your child's high school experience, and homeschoolers have the opportunity to explore a variety of them.

If your child is planning to go to college after high school, the next chapter is packed with college prep advice, including information about AP and dual-enrollment courses and the college application process.

## More Important Than Academics

My greatest hope for all teenagers—even more than being academically successful—is that they develop a deep and personal faith before they launch into independence. The statistics concerning kids growing up in a Christian home and entering college or becoming fully independent are not encouraging. Two-thirds of "churched" kids don't stick with their faith after high school.[1] I am grateful that has not been my kids' experience, but I don't want anyone to assume that homeschooling alone will secure your child's faith. You must be intentional about the time you have and what you focus on as a family (and even then, we know there are no guarantees).

> My greatest hope for all teenagers— even more than being academically successful—is that they develop a deep and personal faith before they launch into independence.

I am convinced that my boys' faith remained solid in college because they became students of the Bible and developed critical thinking skills during their teenage years. They grew in their personal relationship with Jesus and embraced a biblical worldview. Then, while many of their (Christian college) classmates were going through the "deconstruction" of their faith, my boys' roots grew deeper. I don't say this to boast. (My heart breaks for the parents whose kids leave the faith . . . and we can all pray that they will return.) But I say it as encouragement and with a warning. The world won't go easy on our kids if they represent the name of Jesus. And that is why it is important to help our teens know what they believe and why they believe it.

In his book *Revolutionary Parenting: Raising Your Kids to Be Spiritual Champions* (one of my favorite parenting books, by the way), George Barna studies families whose kids had grown up to personally embrace their faith. Barna writes:

> One of the idiosyncrasies of these families is that they tend to delve into faith matters as a family unit. While there are ample instances of family members engaging in spiritual activities apart from other family members—for example, Sunday school classes, small-group involvement, attending Christian events—the glue that holds it all together consists of two themes: family conversations that bring biblical views into their shared lives, and efforts to regularly engage in faith activities (Bible study, worship, prayer) that model the integration of faith into their lives.[2]

I love this so much, and I want to encourage every family to carve out time to make faith a central element of their life. I'm not saying this will be easy just because your kids are homeschooled, but homeschooling will offer you more time together while presenting fewer negative outside influences. I am convinced that homeschooling is the very best way to offer kids the spiritual training and education that will help them launch into the bigger world one day with courage and confidence.

High school is the time for your teenager to discover more of who God made them to be. Cheer your student on to ask questions, to try new things (and sometimes fail!), and to imagine, create, and have fun. This is what homeschooling high school should be all about.

> I am convinced that homeschooling is the very best way to offer kids the spiritual training and education that will help them launch into the bigger world one day with courage and confidence.

Looking back, I have great memories of the years I spent homeschooling my three oldest sons through high school. I had a front-row seat to these boys becoming men. They also became self-directed learners and hard workers. They all began to lead ministries, overcome insecurities, and challenge their own boundaries. During their high school years, my boys became some of my very best friends. I genuinely look forward to all that is ahead with my fourth and final homeschooled son.

As I remember my early years of homeschooling and all my fears, I can only thank God that he gave me the courage to keep going and homeschool all the way through. And I can say with confidence that there is no seven-figure science wing that could be better than the experience we have had homeschooling high school.

## TAKE-HOME THOUGHT

Homeschooling in high school is a great way to prepare your kids for higher education and real-life experiences that require character, faith, and critical-thinking skills.

## REFLECTION QUESTION

Considering how quickly the high school years go by, what are the most important things you want to give your child before they launch?

CHAPTER 9

# THE NITTY-GRITTY

## College Prep

I confess that from the moment I started homeschooling my kids, college was on my mind. It's not that I believe every kid needs to go to college (I don't), but I wanted to be sure that door would be open if my kids wanted to go in that direction. Or at least I wanted to be sure that I wasn't the one closing it. And that felt more than a little scary! (Can anyone relate?)

Hopefully chapter 8 gave you a good idea of what it takes to give your homeschooled child a solid high school education. This chapter focuses on the nitty-gritty of preparing for and applying to college. I'll also talk about taking a gap year between high school and college, which was a great choice for my two oldest sons.

Colleges have specific high school requirements, and this can be the cause of a lot of stress for parents. If your child is interested in a trade school, an apprenticeship, or the military, I highly recommend that you explore suggested coursework or tests for each potential profession or field of study. I've included a list of post–high school career possibilities in the resource section of the book that might be an inspiring springboard for these conversations.

My husband and I had great college experiences, and my husband is a medical doctor, which required college (and a lot more schooling after that), so we have always wanted our boys to have the same opportunity if they chose it. However, I do understand that traditional college is not necessarily the best route for many students. Later in this chapter, I share some statistics about college debt and post-college jobs that will highlight this fact. Meanwhile, I hope this chapter offers all the practical steps needed for those who are keeping the college option open.

No doubt there is a lot to cover on this topic. But my hope is to talk about everything you need to know *while not stressing you out.* I can say honestly that my two oldest sons did most of their college prep work independently—as in, I wasn't hovering over them, reminding them of every step. After we discussed options for their future with them when they were in their early teens, they developed the motivation to go to college, and over time (not overnight) they took on the responsibility for getting there. (I believe their gap year made this much more doable as well!) Though there were stressful moments, overall the college prep process was positive and exciting.

I want to note here that not all kids who say they are interested in college are quick to take on the responsibility for getting there. It may be a process, and some kids will need more support than others. A son or daughter who is not movivated to start this process may be showing you that they are not ready for college. (Again, the gap year idea may be of interest to you if that is the case.) I encourage parents to begin exploring options and having these conversations as early as possible!

# Preparing Your Homeschooled Kids for College

Preparing a student for college will require a bit of teamwork. Like I said, ultimately your student will need to make a personal commitment to pursuing a college education (if that's the direction they choose to go), but initially we, as parents, are likely to open that door. My youngest son shows very little interest in academics at this point, but since I see his potential (he's bright!) and know he currently hopes to pursue a professional golf career, my job is to help him connect the dots between his education today and a college golf scholarship. (I hope he grows to love school too, but: baby steps.) Whether the golf part sticks or not, I'm playing my cards the best I can!

Here are some of the best ways parents can help point their students who have dreams of attending college—or kids who have college potential but aren't quite sure of their future plans—in the right direction.

## Provide College-Prep Coursework

Be intentional about choosing high school coursework that is college preparatory in nature. When my older boys were in high school, I was aware of curriculums that students could get through easily and quickly, and I knew these would be easy As for my boys. But easy classes would not prepare them well for harder college classes, so I decided it would be better for them to "pay up front," as I call it, by taking more challenging classes while in the comfort of their own home. (They thanked me for this later.)

Dave and I also made it clear that our college savings were, ahem, *limited*. Therefore, if the boys hoped to go to an expensive college (which is almost every college), they would need scholarships. We wanted to avoid college debt, so we made their options clear: community college, an affordable college, or a scholarship (combined with some of our college savings). We believed that any of those routes could provide them with a great education. Having this conversation early on motivated our boys to take their high school studies seriously and work to earn those scholarships.

And they did. They put a lot of hours into their school days. They read a lot and stretched their brains to understand complicated equations and difficult concepts. They watched lectures, and when they didn't understand something, *they watched them again.* I wasn't much help with much of their high school curriculum (Calculus? Physics? Not my jam!), so they had to dig in to master the concepts. This might have been one of the best parts of their high school homeschooling. They were learning to learn.

## Visit Prospective Colleges

A great way to motivate your high school students to consider their future is by taking them to visit prospective colleges. Back when Josiah and Jonah were in their early teens, I took them to a few colleges in California. Seeing a college campus bustling with students, getting a peek into the dining hall and on-campus coffee shop, and touring a few of the classrooms and dorms set some college dreams in motion for my boys. Later, as the college years got closer, we toured our local colleges and a community college as well. It is never too early to plant these seeds in a child's mind and, while you're at it, explore entrance requirements and scholarship opportunities. A college visit may also be the inspiration your child needs to work hard throughout high school.

## Prepare for the SAT and/or the ACT

I know some people are anti–standardized testing, and I understand that not all students are natural test takers. I also agree that standardized tests are not necessarily a great measure of a child's intelligence. (In fact, some incredibly gifted students really struggle with standardized tests.) But I still think they are useful. I have given my homeschooled boys a standardized test almost every year, beginning in late elementary or early middle school. This helped me to see areas where they were doing well and areas we needed to focus on in the next year. It also showed me how my kids' scores compared to those of other kids across the country. A couple of my boys were more natural test takers than the others. Some years their scores were lower than I had hoped for (which resulted in a discussion between their dad and me!). Over time we realized that many factors affected their testing, including how rested and healthy they were at the time, any distractions going on around them, and even their mood. As a result of testing each year, the inconsistencies smoothed out and they became more experienced test takers. Instead of avoiding tests, we used the information gained from them to improve our kids' education.

In Hawaii homeschoolers are required to turn in standardized test scores to their local public school while in specific grades. Our local school invited my boys to take the Hawaii standardized test at the school, but I chose to order tests on my own and allow my kids to test at home for convenience. There are options for which tests you can give your kids; over time my boys took the Iowa State Test and the Stanford Achievement Test. (Though the initials are "SAT," it is different from the college-prep SAT, and yes, that can be confusing.) I ordered both tests through the Bob Jones University (BJU) website. To be an official test proctor through BJU, you are required to show that you have a college degree. If you do not have a college degree, you can either test through someone else in your community who is signed up to proctor tests, test at your local school, or find a test that does not have that requirement. (In the resource section, you will find links to sites where you can learn more about giving your kids standardized tests.)

## SAT or ACT?

There is a lot of talk these days about the fact that many colleges no longer require the SAT or ACT. This may be good news for students who don't do well at test taking, but I am convinced that standardized tests will continue to be important for homeschooled students. After all, these tests are one of the only ways to show colleges what a student knows. Schools will be aware that, for a homeschooler, an A from Mom may not be equivalent to an A from an objective teacher. These tests are also very important when you begin to explore college scholarships. Therefore, I think it is wise to plan and prepare your kids to take the SAT, the ACT, or both.

The SAT (originally called the Scholastic Aptitude/Achievement Test) and the ACT (formerly called the American College Testing assessment) have both traditionally been accepted by colleges, and students can generally choose which they prefer to use for admissions.

The ACT covers five core areas: English, math, reading, writing (optional), and science. Students can get practice for the ACT by registering for the PreACT in tenth grade or early in the fall of eleventh grade. You can find many ACT prep courses online.

The SAT covers three core areas: reading, writing and language, and math; plus it has an optional SAT essay (which is required by some colleges). Students can take a pre-SAT (PSAT) test in tenth or eleventh grade. PSAT tests are also offered in eighth or ninth grade. The PSAT is the qualifying test for the National Merit Scholarship Program. You'll find more information about all these testing options at the College Board website.[1]

## How to Prepare for the SAT and ACT

The very best prep for the SAT or ACT begins in the early years with parents reading aloud to kids and kids growing up reading a lot of books. Research shows that kids who are read to consistently as children score better on college entrance exams. But if you're reading this with teenagers in the house, that information may not be very helpful. You can't go back in time, so what can you do now?

There are many study guides and tutorials—both online and in-person prep courses—available at a cost to help students prepare for the SAT and ACT. However, in most cases I don't think it is necessary to pay for anything. Josiah and Jonah used almost only what was free online—primarily the official SAT prep site and the Khan Academy website. At one point, Jonah purchased a prep course online and eventually put it aside and went back to the free methods. Both of my boys would say that these free websites offered them everything they needed to prepare for the tests; it was more about their focused studying than the method used. Jonah, especially, committed a lot of time to his test prep, and it ultimately paid off.

Some students will do better with more guidance, and if that is the case, I think it is worth it to invest in some help. Just be sure that your child is motivated and you are not investing in something you hope will be a magic solution. Kids need to take ownership of their post–high school plans, period. (A gap year may be helpful with this, so hang on for information about that below.)

Most people recommend that students take an initial SAT or ACT test during their junior year of high school. Josiah preferred (and scored better on) the ACT, and Jonah preferred the SAT. Both of them took these tests their junior year and then again their senior year. Josiah improved his score and was in the excellent range (the range listed on college websites for their academic or merit scholarships) on his second ACT and submitted that score to his colleges of interest. He was offered a number of college scholarships and ultimately accepted one to Westmont College as part of their Augustinian Scholars Program (more on that in a bit).

Jonah wanted to continue to improve his score, with the

hope of getting the same scholarship Josiah had received from Westmont, so he took the test again at the end of his senior year. And again that summer. And finally in the fall of his gap year, he took it *one more time.*

I opened chapter 10 of *Raising Amazing* by telling the story of Jonah's grit and determination with his SAT experience. I feel bad admitting that I was not convinced it was worth his time. ("Is it really likely that you'll raise your test score on the fourth attempt?") I even discouraged him from taking the test that one last time.

And, as I shared in *Raising Amazing,* Jonah proved me wrong and improved his test score significantly. And later, when he received his college scholarship, we all knew it had been worth his time. I am still so proud of him! All of that to say that sometimes, with a lot of hard work and focused effort, kids can improve their test scores enough to make a difference in their college options. But the sooner they start preparing, the better.

### Start Earning College Credits—in High School

This is one category where I can invite you to *learn from our mistake.* (You're welcome!) When my first two sons were in high school, I wasn't tuned in to all the opportunities available for them to earn college credits while they were still in high school. They did take a couple of advanced placement (AP) courses and passed the exams (I'll talk more about AP courses below), so that removed a few required college courses, but otherwise they began their college experience with no college credits. Nada. None. I remember talking to them during their first weeks of college, and they told me that almost all their new classmates had taken dual-enrollment classes in high school and had come into college with a semester or two—or more!—of college credit under their belt. (Sorry, boys.) I'd love to help you avoid my mistake, so let's talk about all the ways high school students can get a head start on college.

## *Advanced Placement*

Advanced Placement, or AP, is a program that allows high school students to take higher-level classes and then take an AP exam at the end of the school year. If a student passes the AP exam, they will be able to bypass that class in college. The AP program is run by the College Board, which is the same organization that offers the SAT, and the AP tests are typically held at local high schools at the end of each school year.

The AP exam is scored on a scale of 1 to 5, and while anything above a 3 is considered a "passing" score, colleges vary in what they will accept to bypass a class. (Some will count a 3, while others require a 4 or even a 5.) One of my sons got a 4 on one of his AP exams and a 3 on the other. Westmont accepted only the 4.

The AP program has been around since the 1950s, but it has become more popular in the last few decades. There are now at least thirty-eight different subjects available as AP classes. Different schools offer different AP courses, and while not all AP subjects are available to homeschooled students, it is worth exploring to see if there are any that fall under your child's areas of interest.[2]

A class can be called an AP class on a transcript only if it has been approved by the College Board. You can use the word "honors" or "advanced" to label classes that have not been approved by the College Board but ought to be weighted heavier than a typical high school course. My older boys both took AP calculus, and one of them took AP physics as well. There are not a lot of homeschool curriculums that offer AP-level classes, so my sons were happy to discover that the DIVE/Shormann online curriculum they were already using offered what they wished to take. (And it was excellent!)

Similar to the SAT, students must request that the College Board send their AP scores to the college they want to receive those credits. More information about AP classes and credits can be found on the College Board website.[3] Students are not required to take an AP class to sit the exam, but it is highly recommended. Both boys felt that their AP classes were also great preparation for the college classes they took later.

### Other Testing Options

CLEP tests (also administered by the College Board), DSST (often used by the US military), and the UExcel (through Excelsior College) are other tests a student can take to receive college credits. These are similar to AP tests but also have unique qualities. Links to all of these are included in the resource section.

### Dual-Enrollment Classes

Beginning in their junior year of high school, students can take dual-enrollment classes either online or in person through most colleges. By doing so, they can earn high school credit at the same time as college credit. This makes a lot of sense for homeschoolers who are likely paying for a curriculum in high school anyway. Classes are typically more affordable when taken in dual enrollment than when taken after high school graduation. This is also a great way to give high school students the chance to take a class with a professor and get a taste of what lies ahead in college.

Since I learned my lesson with our first two sons, I encouraged Luke to investigate dual-enrollment classes through Liberty University online before his senior year. He was able to take two dual-enrollment classes while finishing high school and surfing professionally. (I felt a bit of redemption!) Once Luke had officially "graduated" from high school, I learned that the prices of online college classes are much higher than they are for high schoolers taking dual enrollment classes. With this in mind, I recommend taking full advantage of the dual-enrollment option while your kids are still considered high school students.

Many homeschooled students also enjoy attending a community

college in person for dual-enrollment classes. This gives them a taste of the college classroom along with teacher support while also providing them with high school and college credits. Win-win-win!

## High School Transcripts

Potential homeschool parents tend to get squeamish about the topic of high school transcripts—to the extent that the idea of having to create their own is enough to make a lot of parents give up on the idea and send their kids to a traditional school. Don't get discouraged—it really isn't that hard!

If you are keeping a record of your child's courses (with hours/credits as we discussed in the last chapter), then creating a transcript at the end of high school will not be difficult. In fact, it will significantly decrease your stress level to put the transcript together as you go. Many sites offer transcript help or even templates to guide you. For a reasonable price, some services will create an official transcript for you. You'll find more on this in the resource section at the end of the book.

I recommend that, beginning with eighth grade or at least by high school, you write down all that your child is doing academically. It's easier to have too much information—but have all you will need later—than to try to remember later and document it all at once. I know families who scrambled in the final months of their child's senior year to put everything together, and trust me, it was not fun.

We were blessed to work with a Hawaii-based organization called Christian Education Institute (CEI) during my first three boys' high school years. This program offered curriculum planning consultation, transcript preparation, a diploma, and even a graduation ceremony—and their fees were very reasonable. I greatly appreciated CEI's support and encouragement, but they have since closed their doors, so now I am—while wiping away tears—putting on my transcript-creator hat for Levi. As disappointed as I was to lose this service, now that I know about all the available help online, I think it will be a fun adventure to create Levi's transcript on my own.

If you would like to work with someone who will guide you in keeping records and creating a transcript, you have many services to choose from. HSLDA has a transcript service that also calculates GPA (the cost was $24.99 at the time of this writing). A website called Fast Transcripts offers help with creating college-approved transcripts and provides electronic delivery of transcripts, something some colleges now require. (Again, links to everything are found in the resource section of the book.)

## Applying to College

As with all areas of homeschooling, the college application process is not as bad as most people imagine it to be. And, as with most areas of parenting, I suggest you encourage as much independence in this process as possible. If you are a parent who tends to helicopter or micromanage, I want to remind you that you will not be doing your college-bound child any favors. I know a handful of well-intentioned parents who had their hands in every step of their child's high school education and college application process, and those kids had a rude awakening once they went to college. Without Mom there to micromanage their lives, they had a hard time navigating the stressors that came their way.

With that being said, I do recommend that you keep a close eye on the application process and be prepared to coach your student through the entire process (at arm's length, if possible). The earlier you become familiar with the required steps, the better. Most importantly, keep track of dates for various deadlines and then keep in communication with your child, as you will both have responsibilities along the way.

Two aspects of the college application process to be aware of before you start are the Common App and the Counselor Account.

## The Common Application

The Common Application (aka "the Common App") is an online undergraduate application used by more than nine hundred colleges. It simplifies the college application process by allowing students to fill out one application with most of their general information and one main essay, which will go out to the various colleges to which they apply. Beyond what is in the Common App, some colleges will have their own unique essay questions or other specific requests that can be filled out individually. Also, within the online Common App account, students can keep track of other documents that are due (such as letters of recommendation) and all the deadlines. The Common App has simplified the college application process greatly.

## The Counselor Account

Within the Common App there is a Counselor Account section. For students who go to a traditional school, a guidance counselor submits school records as well as their own letter of recommendation to each college on the student's list. However, for homeschooled students, the parent plays the role of guidance counselor, which means *you* will have access to the Counselor Account. This is where you will upload your homeschool transcript, course descriptions, and a letter of recommendation. Some parts of the Counselor Account won't fit perfectly, since this section was created for a traditional high school counselor to fill out, but it is recommended that you fill out those parts however you feel most comfortable. (Don't let the application intimidate you!) I took advantage of this section as an opportunity to talk about my sons' character, unique interests, and even the heart of our homeschooling.

On August 1 of every year, the Common App refreshes for the upcoming application season. Mark this date on your calendar, and know that when your child is a senior, August 1 is when the college application process can begin.[4] If you are anxious about this process (or are just an overachiever), you can go to the Common App website and create a practice account anytime. Feel free to begin this process years ahead of time if you need to. You'll find links to some helpful articles that will walk you through the Common App in the resource section.

As you prepare for the college application process, note that most colleges have an "early application" deadline in the fall. Meeting this deadline can increase a student's chance of acceptance, and early application is required for certain scholarship opportunities (like the one my boys received), so be sure to note these dates on a calendar as well.

All the other details of the college application process will make more sense when you're walking through it. Your child will need some letters of reference, and the sooner you reach out to potential references, the better. My sons had a variety of people offer letters of reference: Josiah had his boss from his freshman-year internship, as well as a church youth pastor, write his references. Jonah had Dr. Shormann of DIVE curriculum, whom he had begun working for, as well as his speech and debate coach. If your kids are staying busy with community involvement and extracurriculars, they will have no problem finding options for letters of reference (coaches, mentors, instructors).

### Consider a Gap Year

I don't remember where I first heard the idea of a gap year, but during Josiah's senior year, we started to discuss a gap year for a few reasons. First, he was going to graduate a bit young. (He had skipped a grade somewhere in middle school and would graduate as a seventeen-year-old.) Also, as I have mentioned, we weren't exactly sure about his college plan, and I felt unprepared and thought we could use more time.

Josiah liked the idea of a gap year. He was able to enjoy his senior year without the stress of college applications. He dedicated much of the summer and fall after his high school graduation to working on college applications (and fruitless smaller scholarship applications, which I will mention later). He worked many evenings a week at a restaurant, saving up a lot of money, and he was involved in youth ministry. I believe that the mental "gap" in Josiah's gap year gave him space to do an excellent job on his college essays, which played a big part in his earning a significant college scholarship. By the time he left for college the following year, he was a mature young man, ready to soar. Jonah chose to do the same thing, and he used his gap year to take his final SAT test, which, as I shared, made all the difference in his college path.

Many programs and opportunities are offered for students who are taking gap years. I have heard of great yearlong mentorships, mission opportunities, and work/life transitional programs that are worth looking into. Some of these are geared toward students who are struggling, while others are perfect for kids who are ministry-minded or just want to see the world or need a break from academics. Taking a breather between high school and college can be beneficial for a student in many ways. The good news is, if your child does apply for college during their senior year and gets accepted, most colleges will "defer" their college acceptance for one to two years, giving them time to take a gap year with the assurance that they have a college acceptance on hold for when they are ready.

## Finances and Applying for Scholarships

The cost of college can be outrageous, giving families good reason to consider other options. If college is on your and your child's mind, then the sooner you start exploring financial options, the better off you'll be.

Unfortunately, many students graduate from college with overwhelming debt. The Education Data Initiative showed these values from May 2023:

- The average federal student loan debt is **$37,338** per borrower.
- Private student loan debt averages **$54,921** per borrower.
- The average student borrows **over $30,000** to pursue a bachelor's degree.
- A total of **45.3 million** borrowers have student loan debt; **92%** of them have federal loan debt.
- Twenty years after entering school, half of the student borrowers still owe **$20,000** each on outstanding loan balances.[5]

These statistics are especially sad considering how few college graduates find work in their field of study or make enough money to pay back their loans quickly. One recent survey of college graduates from 2021 showed that

- 28% of recent college graduates are working at jobs that require only a high school diploma; 6% have jobs with no education requirements at all;
- 84% of recent grads say finding a job was "very" or "somewhat" difficult; and
- 40% of recent grads still seeking employment have lowered their salary expectations.[6]

You may want to research financial options such as scholarships, grants, and other forms of funding. Keep in mind that in addition to the cost of tuition, students need to consider room and board, books, supplies, personal expenses, and transportation. Some of the options for college funding you might explore include

- state scholarships based on test scores;
- merit-based scholarships for high GPAs, SAT/ACT scores, etc.;
- athletic scholarships for specific sports;* and
- financial aid, including loans, grants, work-study, and tuition assistance.

*A note about athletic scholarships: As you explore scholarship options, keep in mind that currently Division 1, Division 2, and NAIA schools offer athletic scholarships, but Division 3 schools do not.

When Josiah was applying to colleges, we tried to figure out how he might receive smaller scholarships, which, we were told, went unclaimed every year. We spent countless hours looking into scholarships he might qualify for—based on everything from growing up in Hawaii to being a nonsmoker to having exercise-induced asthma. He wrote essays, tweeted anti-smoking campaign messages (required for one particular scholarship), and filled out countless applications, all to no avail. Perhaps we did something wrong, but by the time Jonah was applying to college, we decided to skip that process altogether. (If you know the secret to getting those obscure scholarships, please let me know.)

Depending on a student's grades and test scores, most colleges offer various scholarships that will help shave off at least some tuition. You'll find a list of potential scholarships at each college website, and the earlier you discover what is available, the sooner your child might be motivated to work hard in high school.

When Josiah was applying to colleges, we learned just in time that some private Christian colleges offer a unique scholarship based on a combination of grades, test scores, and faith/character/community involvement. Since Westmont College was one of Josiah's favorites, we were thrilled to discover that they had an Augustinian Scholars Program, which seemed to be an excellent fit for him. This is how the program is described:

> The Augustinian Scholars Program (ASP) offers a four-year scholarship and honors curriculum to students committed to academic excellence and Christian formation. The ASP invites students to study the work of St. Augustine of Hippo and other key thinkers in the Christian intellectual tradition because a rigorous pursuit of truth grows out of our pursuit of God.[7]

Josiah was introduced by phone to a current Augustinian scholar, and we learned that the credentials to get the scholarship were as follows:

- Profess a commitment to the Christian faith and a desire to grow spiritually.
- Submit excellent academic credentials.
- SAT/ACT recommended (but not required).
- Commit to spending a semester studying abroad.
- Take an interest in and show an aptitude for leadership; demonstrated leadership experience in high school, church and/or volunteer activities desirable.[8]

Josiah applied to Westmont during early admission, and we prayed hard. For this particular scholarship, the process involves Westmont inviting 120 qualified students to the campus during the winter of their senior year to spend a weekend attending meetings, taking part in an essay-writing session, doing group or one-on-one interviews, and enjoying a banquet ceremony. The students sleep in the dorm rooms of current Augustinian scholars, eat some meals in the cafeteria, and get to attend a college class. Students are evaluated by the admissions team, as well as by current Augustinians, and a few weeks later 60 incoming first-year students are offered the Augustinian Scholarship.

A few weeks after Josiah turned in his application, just before the Christmas holidays, he received an envelope inviting him to the Augustinian contest weekend. We were thrilled! He had a great time at the scholarship contest weekend, and then we held our breath for two weeks until he received the much-anticipated phone call from the Westmont admissions team. As I mentioned previously, not only did Josiah end up receiving the scholarship and enjoying four years as an Augustinian scholar (he loved poring over Augustine's writings as well as the work of C. S. Lewis and other writers and thinkers, with stimulating discussions and other unique academic opportunities), but two years later, Jonah also became an Augustinian scholar.

While we are super grateful for how things worked out for our boys, we know that there are many avenues to receiving a college degree. We know people who have gotten there in a great variety of ways. I am also confident that my boys would have thrived in any college setting in which God might have placed them.

> As parents we may get caught up in checklists and timelines, but ultimately God will work everything out when we focus on shaping the hearts and character of our kids.

I say this as I recall an unforgettable moment with Josiah during his college application process. One day, after touring a local college on the island, we were walking through Chinatown in Honolulu looking for a place to eat lunch.

I was feeling all kinds of stress about his college options and his future. I asked his forgiveness for introducing him to all the fancy California colleges when the truth was, we couldn't afford any of them. I was trying to warm him up to the idea of community college. As a mom, I was feeling a bit lost.

We stopped on the street corner, and Josiah turned to me with a smile and said, "Mom, let's not make too big of a deal about where I go to college. Here's the thing: Wherever I go, I will get an education. I will find community. God will take care of me. It's going to be fine."

What a blessing his words were to his stressed-out mom! I knew at that point that his homeschooling experience might have prepared him academically for college, but even better, I knew that I had raised a son with a mature perspective and a faith that challenged my own. We found some good saimin noodles, and I felt the weight lift off my shoulders.

As parents we may get caught up in checklists and timelines, but ultimately God will work everything out when we focus on shaping the hearts and character of our kids.

## TAKE-HOME THOUGHT

Preparing your homeschooler for their future will require time and hard work, but the eventual rewards will exceed your efforts as your child soars into all that is ahead.

## REFLECTION QUESTION

Which area of college prep seems most overwhelming, and what work might you do to begin to tackle next steps in that area?

PART III

EVERYTHING
ELSE YOU NEED
TO KNOW

CHAPTER 10

# BEYOND CORE CURRICULUM

## Electives and Extracurriculars

Whatever your school experience was growing up, I imagine you'd agree that academics were just one part of your overall school experience. Likely, many of your school memories come from things you did outside of the classroom. That is true from my own experience growing up in the public school system.

Much of the homeschool experience is also what happens outside of core academics. When I asked my adult sons to share their top memories from high school, Josiah's first response was, "Stargazing from our front lawn after dinner—mapping the stars with Dad and the bros is one of my favorite memories, hands down." Other responses included surfing, skateboarding, spearfishing, speech and debate club (Jonah), creating stop-motion videos, birding with Dad, being on the worship team for youth group, game nights with friends, and the list goes on.

I am grateful for all the opportunities homeschoolers have to grow up to be well-rounded people with unique interests and skills and a social aptitude that will take them far in this world.

In this chapter, we will look at the opportunities homeschoolers have beyond their core academics, and I'll talk about my top-recommended electives and extracurricular activities, as well as how you can turn extracurriculars into elective credits. (*Boom!*) With a little intention, homeschooled kids will have the opportunity to take much more than a high school transcript with them into the world when they graduate.

## Elective Classes and Extracurricular Activities

When it comes to homeschooling, sometimes it can be difficult to differentiate between high school electives and extracurricular activities, and for good reason: they often overlap. In the earlier years of homeschooling, there isn't a need to separate the two. Kids can pursue interests and passions to their hearts' content. However, once they are in high school, you are wise to keep track of the things they are investing a lot of time in, as they have the potential to be counted as elective credits on their high school transcript.

An *elective* can be defined as a class outside of a student's core academics that has some form of academic content. An *extracurricular* is any activity outside of official schoolwork that a student participates in and will be helpful to include on college applications.

### High School Electives

Homeschoolers can use elective classes to develop their God-given passions and interests, explore career opportunities, and develop life skills. Depending on your state requirements, most high schoolers take one to three electives each year, and homeschoolers can take advantage of this requirement to add some flavor and fun to their core academics.

While electives are one area of homeschooling you might enjoy allowing your student to choose on their own, I do recommend guiding them to choose well. I give my sons a few required categories to choose from, as well as a few that are completely up to them. So if they take a total of ten electives during high

> Homeschoolers can use elective classes to develop their God-given passions and interests, explore career opportunities, and develop life skills.

school, five of them will be in a required category, while the other five are led by their own interests.

## Elective Categories I Recommend

### 1. Money management

Personal finance doesn't come up in most high school classes, but it may be one of the most important topics a student can learn before launching into independence. More than 80 percent of Americans are in debt, and college students and young adults, who tend to be short on money, are prime targets for credit card companies.

I have confessed that we didn't do a lot to teach our boys about personal finance, but when my oldest son was a senior in high school, our whole family went through Dave Ramsey's Financial Peace University online program. From the very first week, Josiah was captivated. This began his personal journey of learning more about saving, investing, and pursuing a debt-free financial future. He has gone on to learn a lot about all these things and is well on his way to a fine-looking retirement already. (I'm a little jealous.) There are many excellent online resources for students who want to study personal finance during high school, and some of these are listed in the resource section.

## 2. Foreign language

Not all high schools require foreign language credits to graduate, but most colleges require two years of foreign language. Even if a student doesn't think they are college-bound, I think it is wise to keep that door open, so even if it's not a required course, I highly recommend foreign language as an elective. Though spoken languages are most often used for this credit, I have heard of colleges that accept sign language classes for the foreign language requirement. I steered my boys toward a language that would be practical for their future (they chose Japanese, Spanish, and French), and you will find many online options for foreign language classes for homeschoolers as well as local community college classes and other group classes or conversation groups they can enroll in or join.

## 3. Biblical worldview

As kids leave our home, they will be entering a post-Christian culture, which is mostly not in alignment (to say it kindly) with a biblical worldview. Research by Barna shows that in America, nearly two-thirds of eighteen- to twenty-nine-year-olds who grew up active in church turn away from their faith as adults.[1]

Even my oldest sons who went to a private Christian college (which they loved) watched several students go through the "deconstruction" of their faith while at college.[2] If our kids don't know what they believe and why they believe it, they will be incredibly vulnerable to the confusing and counterbiblical messages being presented by their teachers, peers, and the culture around them. I highly recommend that all Christian families make biblical worldview, critical thinking, and apologetics required subjects in their high schoolers' education.

4. **Fine arts**

All kids benefit greatly from learning some basic music and art skills. I am not gifted in either of these areas, but I am glad my husband has made them a priority. We started our oldest sons in piano lessons during elementary school, and by high school one of them was a gifted guitar player and the other had stuck with piano. Both used their giftings to lead worship in their youth group, and music followed them into their college years. Luke, who also took piano, set it aside for years but has recently been teaching himself ukulele, so I'd like to believe the piano background contributed to that. Levi has also dabbled in ukulele, and he loves music, so I'm hopeful that will develop over time.

Even if a child isn't drawn to music or art, they may find a connection to theater, dance, or other fine arts, which can be a great part of their high school experience and can lead to future opportunities in college or elsewhere.

5. **Computer coding (or other technology education)**

Tech giant Mark Zuckerberg has famously said, "All of my friends who have younger siblings who are going to college or high school—my number one piece of advice is: you should learn how to program."[3] Josiah studied data analytics in college and got a job working with data and computer coding straight out of school. He agrees with Mark Zuckerberg that every child should learn computer coding; in his opinion, coding is more important than a foreign language. Whether or not we agree with that, we cannot deny that our world is becoming more and more technologically driven, and a student will benefit from having some type of foundation in and knowledge of technology.

This is by no means an exhaustive list of electives. You might swap out one of mine or add to the list other courses that are important to you. Additional electives that are high on my list are cooking, car maintenance, gardening, woodworking, and other practical life skills.

## Assigning Credits for Electives

To assign credits for electives, you can follow the same basic guidelines discussed in chapter 8. Though there are a few ways to determine credits (more on that in the resource section!) it is wise to record how many hours your student spends on a subject, and assign credit hours accordingly. (One credit hour is typically 150-180 hours, with additional hours for classes with labs or Advanced Placement classes.[4] But *always* check your state laws to make sure.) As with other classes, if your student spends an hour most weekdays of the school year on the subject (or the equivalent of that), then by the end of the year they will have earned one credit.[5] Grading on these classes will be more subjective, but you can decide how best to evaluate their learning. Just like in a traditional school, you as the teacher have some freedom in how you choose to organize and evaluate elective classes.

One of my homeschool mom friends reminded me that electives can be helpful in boosting a student's GPA. The As her daughter earned through electives helped counterbalance lower grades in classes she struggled more in. She gave her daughter school credits for an SAT prep class, driver's ed, a part-time job (which fulfilled a "life skills" credit), and a dance class that she spent well over 180 hours in during the year. Smart mom.

## Extracurriculars

Extracurriculars can be anything from an internship or job to sports, ministry, community service, or just about anything a student does with their free time. Homeschoolers have a ton of freedom to pursue extracurricular activities, and there is space for up to ten extracurricular activities on the Common App. In fact, colleges like to see a résumé full of strong extracurricular activities, and a student's list of extracurriculars gives schools an idea of their interests and initiative, leadership qualities, and how much they might contribute to the college campus.

It's also possible to turn many extracurricular activities into elective classes by tracking the hours spent doing the activity and making sure there is an educational element to it. As you guide your student to find the best extracurricular activities, this list of questions might be helpful:

> A student's list of extracurriculars gives schools an idea of their interests and initiative, leadership qualities, and how much they might contribute to the college campus.

1. **What is my student naturally drawn to?**

    Encourage your child to follow their passions. If they love nature and the outdoors, consider opportunities in your community where they might join a hiking club or volunteer at a nature reserve. If your student is interested in music, you can invest in lessons, encourage them to join or start a music club, or suggest that they join the worship team at church. (My sons started out as worship leaders for the middle school youth group.)

2. **What area does my student need to grow or be stretched in?**

    If your child is naturally shy or reserved, you might find a club or group that would give them a comfortable place to develop more social skills. If you find that your student is acting selfish or entitled, then signing them up for a volunteer role at a nursing home or food bank might be a life-changing experience. Our current culture encourages kids to be self-focused, with an emphasis—via entertainment and social media—on being *oh-so-me-centered*. Regularly serving others can be helpful to counteract this.

3. **What is reasonable for our family's values and schedule?**

In the second chapter of my book *Raising Amazing*, I talk about the importance of knowing and communicating your family values and the idea of creating a family mission statement. As you discuss what each of your kids will commit time to, it is wise to ask, "Does this activity fit with what we value most as a family? Is this a good use of our time? Will adding this activity be a blessing or cause more stress to our family's schedule?" Sometimes, due to what we think we need to do (or good ol' FOMO), we load our kids' days with so many activities that we forget about downtime and family time, which are big parts of why we started home-schooling to begin with.

I saw a homeschool friend recently who confessed that the previous school year, in all her enthusiasm to be "the great homeschool mom," she completely overbooked her kids with "enriching" activities. A few months into running around to classes and clubs most days of the week, her kids were exhausted and she felt more like "the burned-out homeschool mom" than anything else. She was looking forward to the new school year ahead, in which she planned to spend a lot of time at home and enroll her kids in only a select few activities that would truly enrich their lives. There are endless options for extracurricular activities, and you will find a list of more ideas in the resource section. Just remember: choosing well is the key!

## Colleges Care about Extracurriculars

Colleges look for high-quality extracurriculars in homeschooled applicants. They are aware that homeschooled students have more freedom with their time, and they expect to see that students have been investing their time well. Colleges also love to find applicants who have interesting and unique extracurriculars, especially those with leadership elements. They want to have a diverse and well-rounded group of incoming students, and homeschoolers do a great job of strengthening their student population.

When my oldest sons were in high school, an older friend who had been homeschooled and was then in college at Biola University shared advice from his own experience. He said that colleges are looking for leadership, so it's a good idea to turn something you love and already do into a club of which you are the president or leader. Following that advice, Jonah started a "surf and Bible" club, where he invited friends to do a short Bible study with him each week before a group surf session. He organized the group, brought snacks, and led the Bible study. This was a great experience for him, other kids loved it, and it was a helpful addition to his college résumé.

The CollegeVine website has this to say about homeschoolers who hope to go to college and the importance of extracurriculars:

> Colleges seek initiative, creativity, and independence much more in the home schooled applicant than in the traditional applicant. The unique structure of a home school education allows for students to pursue extracurricular pursuits, be it business, academic competitions, or community service, to a degree their peers can't. Colleges want to ensure that students have taken advantage of this opportunity, so students who can demonstrate strong themes of leadership and inventiveness in their applications have a strong shot at admissions to the nation's most competitive schools.[6]

## Internships and Jobs

One benefit of homeschooling is that kids are available to get work experience during the school day when most students are stuck in a classroom. Many local businesses would love to have a teenager help out a day or two a week, and you can even give your student academic credits if they spend enough hours on the job.

Josiah interned for Eric Arakawa, a surfboard shaper (someone who designs and builds surfboards), during his freshman year of high school. He spent about four hours in the shop two times a week, learning about the business, as well as sweeping the shop and helping out in many other ways. In exchange for his work, Eric gave him credit toward a new surfboard (they're not cheap!). At the end of the semester, Josiah received a new surfboard, as well as an official certificate of completion. I was able to give him half a credit for "business internship" on his transcript. And when it was time for Josiah to apply for college, Eric was happy to write a recommendation based on Josiah's time spent working for him.

Another fun connection occurred when we met David Shormann, the founder and professor of the online math and science homeschool curriculum Shormann Math and DIVE into Math and Science. Dr. Shormann and his family had moved to our North Shore community from Texas, and his homeschooled daughter was involved in the youth group our older boys went to. Dr. Shormann became a mentor to our boys, and he invited many of the students (and families!) onto his boat to dive with dolphins, do some spearfishing, and test out his whale fin–inspired surfboard fin design.

As Dr. Shormann got to know my sons, he noted their interest in math and science and saw that they did well with his curriculum. Eventually he offered each of them opportunities to work with him. They both helped with research on his patented "whale fin" technology, and Jonah later worked as an editor for Dr. Shormann's new Calculus II curriculum. I love how God can provide connections and opportunities in your own community. Keep praying. Keep exploring. And trust him with the rest.

Though the experience with Dr. Shormann was excellent for their college résumés (and gave them some of their best ocean memories), I must note that my boys benefited in different, but also important, ways from working at a local restaurant. Both Josiah and Jonah worked at Lei Lei's restaurant on the Turtle Bay Resort golf course for their last year of high school and during their gap year. Doing dishes and busing tables in an intense restaurant environment provided them with "character growth," whether they were looking for it or not. They also developed greater motivation for furthering their education!

Both colleges and trade schools will want to see that students have demonstrated interest, achievement, dedication, and leadership skills during their homeschool years. It is extremely helpful for students to show that they have pursued activities outside of the classroom and that they will be a positive asset to the college campus.[7]

Enjoy the process of offering your student a variety of opportunities to grow as a well-rounded individual, a hard worker, and a creative problem solver. Some of these things will require extra effort on your part. You may need to drive your child to meetings, lessons, or a job. Coordinating schedules may be challenging. But keep this in mind: You are giving your children so much more than an academic education. You are giving them experiences, adventures, and windows into brand-new worlds—along with the opportunity to meet a variety of people. You are helping them to develop character and passion. You are providing them with a lifetime of memories. You are giving them a life they will thank you for later.

## TAKE-HOME THOUGHT

One of the greatest parts of your kids' homeschool experience will be the opportunities you give them outside of their academics. Have fun making those memories.

## REFLECTION QUESTION

What interest or hobby might you help your child turn into an elective or extracurricular class?

CHAPTER 11

# GOOD AND HEALTHY

## Sports for Homeschoolers

Sports are a huge part of our family's life—and our favorite extracurricular activity. I can't imagine a day in our home without someone training for, competing in, or at least talking about or watching some kind of sport. If you are a sports-loving family, then this chapter is especially for you. We'll discuss some of the specifics of homeschoolers participating in individual and team sports. But first, I want every reader to be reminded: while not every child is destined to be a competitive athlete, being active and fit is an important part of a well-rounded life. So I encourage *all* families to include some sort of physical activity in their kids' schedule. Every year!

## Make Fitness a Priority

Obesity is at epidemic levels for youth in the United States. As of 2019, about 17 percent of US children were presenting with obesity.[1] And we know that obesity impacts kids' psychological and cardiovascular health, as well as their social life, sleep, and so much more. Global research looking at eleven- to seventeen-year-old school-going children in 146 countries, territories, and areas in 2016 found that youth were insufficiently physically active, and experts agree that things have only gotten worse post-pandemic.[2] There is no doubt this corresponds to increased screen time and all our technological advances, but whatever is to blame, the fact remains that it is a problem. Not only are kids who are sedentary establishing patterns they are likely to carry with them into adulthood, but their health will be impacted by the choices they make in their youth as well. A combination of a poor diet and a sedentary lifestyle means that many kids are collecting levels of plaque in their arteries that used to be associated only with unhealthy middle-aged people.

Kids need to exercise. The World Health Organization recommends that children ages five to seventeen get "moderate to vigorously intense" exercise each day for at least sixty minutes. They also recommend that children spend no more than two hours a day on screens for recreational purposes. These recommendations are focused on improving kids' physical and mental health and cognitive abilities.[3] And I don't think we need data to prove this, because anyone who has been around a child who has spent time exercising knows that physical activity absolutely improves their mood and their ability to focus (hello, schoolwork!), while also helping them to sleep better.

Homeschooling families can offer kids the healthy lifestyle of exercise they need. While kids who attend traditional school may be required to sit at a desk all day long (plus, many public schools have eliminated PE and most recesses due to budget cuts), homeschoolers have many options to get active. Making regular movement and fitness a normal and required part of your kids' day is one of the greatest gifts you can give them. Even if they don't appreciate it in the moment, they will thank you for it later.

Besides the organized sports we'll cover below, there are many things kids can do to incorporate exercise into their daily lives. We have turned part of our garage into a workout zone with hand weights, bands, and a stationary bike. Even if you don't have much space available, you can do a lot with dumbbells or other basic equipment. You can use exercise videos (there are great apps and online workouts available, targeting all different age groups) or get creative and make up your own workout routine. You can get out for walks, runs, or bike rides together as a family. Many towns have wonderful gyms that offer family memberships so that everyone can disperse to their favorite activity, class, or kids' club and meet up after everyone has done their own workout.

Besides designated workouts, it is healthy and helpful to incorporate movement throughout your student's day as well. Between classes I often ~~push~~ nudge Levi out the door to go run some laps around the house or play with the dog. He sometimes does his math lessons while standing at our kitchen counter (like a stand-up desk, kid-style), and all my boys have listened to lectures while stretching or doing other activities. In fact, fiddling with a stress ball or doing some other (mindless) activity can help a child focus. A minute or two of jumping jacks or push-ups can be a great refresher or wakeup on sleepy days. (This goes for us parents too!)

As you introduce your kids to a variety of physical activities, there's a good chance that something will begin to stick, and you can look into ways to develop that interest even further. If your child loves to run or swim, look into local track clubs or road races or swim teams. You never know—that interest might lead them to competing in triathlons or marathons one day. One of my (home-schooling) friends took her son bowling for fun, and he ended up loving it and joining a bowling league in high school. Keep an open mind, introduce your child to a variety of activities, and see what happens.

Being married to a hospital physician, I am so aware of the importance of living a healthy lifestyle, and I want to encourage every family to continue—or maybe to begin for the very first time—to prioritize healthy lifestyle choices. Moms and dads: this advice is for you too. Not only will you feel better if you are getting some exercise regularly and eating healthy foods, but know that your kids are watching and taking note—and they are likely to follow in your footsteps.

## Homeschooling and Organized Sports

While I encourage every family to have an active lifestyle, some of you have kids who will be interested in participating in organized sports. Organized sports offer so much to kids: building discipline and dedication, training with a coach, learning teamwork and other social skills, and having many opportunities to develop character.

### Homeschoolers and Individual Sports

Individual sports are a great option for homeschoolers. Homeschooled students can train any time of day and plan their schooling and sports schedules in whatever way works best for them. If their sport involves travel, homeschoolers are blessed with a lot of freedom for that. As a professional surfer, Luke is grateful that homeschooling gave him an advantage in his freedom to train—a lot—from a young age. Levi is getting quite serious about golf, and thus far homeschooling is serving his passion well. As I write, we are preparing to travel to Scottsdale, Arizona, for a regional PGA "Drive, Chip, and Putt" event, and we get to turn it into a weeklong vacation with my parents, thanks to homeschooling.

## Homeschoolers and Team Sports

Team sports have more nuance for homeschoolers. For students who are serious about team sports, especially those hoping to play a team sport in college, taking part in their chosen sport as a homeschooler can be a bit trickier. As with many areas of homeschooling, the laws will vary from state to state (and sometimes from school district to school district), so you will likely have to do some research on this topic and plan to be an advocate for your child. I've heard of many different scenarios from a variety of states, but I'll do my best to give a broad overview of how things look for homeschoolers playing team sports.

The unfortunate truth is, in some states, homeschooled students do not have the same opportunities that their traditionally schooled peers have to play team sports. This is because certain team sports (such as football and basketball) are provided almost exclusively through public or private schools. Since some states do not allow homeschoolers to compete on public school teams, homeschoolers who love team sports can find themselves in a frustrating position.

The Equal Opportunity for Access in Education Act, also referred to as the Tim Tebow bill, was created for this very reason. This bill is named after Tim Tebow, a Heisman Trophy winner who was homeschooled throughout K–12 and went on to play professional football and baseball. (He's also one of my top-recommended authors and role models for kids of all ages and young adults!) The Tim Tebow bill provides homeschooled students access to public school sports. So far, over half of the states in the US now allow homeschooled students to participate in public school sports *to some extent*. I've heard varying information about the status of this bill, so it is best to check your own state's laws to find out if your student would benefit from this and whether any limitations or requirements come with it.

Thankfully, many homeschooled students are welcomed onto public school teams, facing no obstacles whatsoever. I have friends whose homeschooled kids very seamlessly participated in team sports via their local public school, then went on to swim or play volleyball in college.

At this time, Hawaii has not embraced the Tim Tebow bill, and all districts in Hawaii prohibit homeschooled students from participating in public school sports. That has been a frustration for our family, especially Jonah, who wanted to participate on the high school track and soccer teams. Even if your state, like ours, does not allow homeschooled students to participate in public school sports, it's still a good idea to reach out to your local school athletic director to inquire about the possibilities available. Who knows if a few squeaky wheels might help bring new opportunities to homeschooled students across our nation.

I have friends in California whose homeschooled kids happily participate in public high school sports. My friend in Tennessee, who recently started homeschooling her now ninth-grade son, discovered that he had options to participate on a baseball team via a private or public school. She also described a highly competitive baseball team out of Nashville that is comprised of only homeschooled kids. My friend has discovered, however, that there are certain eligibility requirements for participating on each type of team, so her best advice is to research your state homeschool laws and your local athletic association's eligibility requirements. Starting this process before your kids begin high school is a very good idea.

## Club Sports for Homeschoolers

Besides school sports, some sports—such as soccer, swimming, and volleyball—have excellent club teams available, which will attract college scouts. Competing on a club team is an excellent option for homeschoolers, as the clubs function separately from the public school system. Homeschoolers can take full advantage of club teams, which might include a significant amount of time dedicated to travel or tournaments. This time commitment can be challenging for traditionally schooled students, but homeschoolers can make it work well.

## College Athlete Hopefuls

If your child hopes to play NCAA Division 1 or 2 or NAIA sports in college, you will want to check the National Collegiate Athletic Association (NCAA) or the National Association of Intercollegiate Athletics (NAIA) website for eligibility requirements. This information will include all the fees, standardized test scores, official transcripts, other documentation, and everything else needed related to their eligibility to play college sports. (You can find the link in the resource section.) I know I have mentioned it a lot, but the HSLDA website will be very helpful to you too. Also, if your child is expressing interest in playing a collegiate sport—and seems to have the talent and determination to do so—begin looking into the NCAA eligibility by eighth or ninth grade so you can plan ahead.

Whether your child is a competitive athlete or not, homeschooling provides kids with a great opportunity to be physically active, try new sports and fitness activities, and develop an active lifestyle that will last a lifetime. One of the greatest gifts we can give our kids is a healthy start to life—and exercise is a huge part of that.

## TAKE-HOME THOUGHT

Giving your child the foundation of healthy habits and the opportunity to participate in sports and fitness is a gift that will benefit them for the rest of their life.

# REFLECTION QUESTION

Where might you add more movement to your child's days, and how can you help them incorporate more health and fitness activities into their homeschool experience?

CHAPTER 12

# VARIATIONS ON HOMESCHOOLING

## Co-ops, Charter Schools, and Hybrid Schools

With a growing number of families choosing to homeschool, more and more options are available for how a family might go about it. I get a lot of questions from parents trying to make sense of various educational options. From independent homeschooling to participation in a homeschool co-op, to charter programs and hybrid options... the list goes on. All of this could make a potential homeschool parent's head spin. No stress—I'm here to help sort it all out!

Let's begin with a simple definition of homeschooling:

> **Homeschool:** to teach school subjects
> to one's children at home.[1]

Considering this definition, most of the options above might be defined as "homeschooling" to various degrees. If your child is doing school outside of the conventional classroom, at least part of the time, you might call that "homeschooling." And while our family has loved being independent homeschoolers (with some co-op involvement), I will cheer on any family who finds creative ways to spend more time at home together—however they might do that.

In this chapter, I give a quick overview of various homeschooling options, and once again I provide links to helpful resources for each of them at the end of the book. Before I dive in, however, I want to acknowledge that as homeschooling is quickly growing in popularity, there will likely be even more options popping up after this book goes to press. Also, there will always be a lot of variation from state to state in homeschool options and laws. I'll do my best here to address the main homeschooling options at this time and, most importantly, give you some principles to keep in mind that will apply to any methods of homeschooling that might be available.

## Homeschool Co-ops

A homeschool co-op is a community-run group that organizes meetings where students take classes or do other activities together. Co-ops are often led by parents, though in some situations parents pitch in to pay for a teacher or activity leader. Co-ops range from being small and casual to large and highly organized. They meet in churches, homes, or other gathering places. (Some meet outdoors at a park or other nature-centered location.) Most co-ops meet weekly or bimonthly, but the options are endless because it is completely up to the families running them. Co-ops might offer any number of classes, and students can typically choose how involved they want to be.

Most co-ops use a variety of curriculums, though some are based on a single curriculum. The best example of a curriculum-focused co-op is Classical Conversations. "CC" groups meet around the world in homes, churches, and other locations, and they use a branded curriculum based on the classical education model.

Some co-ops are less academic and more oriented toward enrichment, art, or field trips. These organizations are often called a "homeschool group" or "club" instead of a co-op. Students might gather for art or language classes, or to learn specific skills that might not be as easy to do at home (think gardening, auto mechanics, or baking), with one parent responsible to teach from their personal skill set. There are also a lot of homeschool groups whose main purpose is to take regular field trips, go on hikes, or participate in other adventures together.

### Is a Homeschool Co-op Right for You?

Homeschool co-ops are like every other aspect of homeschooling: completely up to your student and your family's preferences. Some people love being involved in a co-op and cannot imagine homeschooling without one. Others are not at all interested in joining one and feel like it would cramp the very style that attracted them to homeschooling in the first place. Others, like me, might enjoy co-ops in certain seasons but not stick with them for the long haul. If you are just beginning to homeschool and have concerns about your child's social development, a co-op could be a really great choice for your family.

If you know of a co-op near you, you might reach out to the leadership and ask if you can bring your student(s) and visit for a day. You can also talk to other co-op members to ask about their experience. While every co-op will be unique, I do think they can be very beneficial for the right students and families.

### Our Co-op Experience

When my first three sons were nine, seven, and five, we joined a local homeschool co-op held at our small North Shore church. It was parent led and very casual. I liked it for the chance to gather with other families and for the social outlet I craved. The boys participated in an art class, science class, and public speaking class, and it was a good experience. We were involved with the co-op for two to three years until the boys' other schoolwork began taking up more time and our schedule was overall just too busy (by then Levi was a baby). I'd still love to get Levi involved in a co-op, but we have gotten comfortable with our fully independent schedule, so thus far we have not been motivated to join one again.

### Find a Homeschool Co-op Near You

If you are interested in joining a homeschool co-op, it may be easiest simply to search for one online in your community. If you have a local homeschool organization, it ought to have a list of available co-ops. The HSLDA website is a good resource for exploring any co-ops that might be meeting in your state. And if you don't find a great fit in a local homeschool co-op, you might consider starting one yourself. There are no rules for how a co-op must look, and if you link arms with a few other families, you might just form the co-op of your dreams.

## Tutorials and Other Variations of Private Homeschool Support

In some communities, you will find a great variety of options for homeschooling with the added support of tutors or professional teachers. These often have a similar feel to a co-op in that they are privately run and often organized by a group of parents. The difference is that most of these utilize a paid "teacher" who works with a group of students or one-on-one. Some of these are packaged under the name "academy" or "tutorial," and they most often meet one or two days a week, with the students doing the bulk of their work at home. I imagine that over time groups like this will become more and more popular and might be an excellent option for homeschool families who want to offer their kids a college-preparatory education, specialized teachers, and an intentional social environment, while still spending the majority of their school hours at home.

## Charter Schools

The National Charter School Resource Center defines a charter school like this:

> A charter school is a public school that operates as a school of choice. Charter schools commit to obtaining specific educational objectives in return for a charter to operate a school. Charter schools are exempt from significant state or local regulations related to operation and management but otherwise adhere to regulations of public schools—for example, charter schools cannot charge tuition or be affiliated with a religious institution.[2]

As the website states, a charter school is a form of *public school*. Since two of the top reasons my husband and I have chosen to homeschool our kids are to offer them a Bible-based education (with Christian values throughout all the subjects) and not to depend on the government for our kids' education, I have never considered using a charter school. However, I want to talk about charter schools here for three reasons.

First, some states/districts give enough freedom to families in their charter programs that their experience is very close to homeschooling. I know families in California and Texas who have used Christian curriculum for some of their subjects, as long as the sample work they show their "homeschool advisor" isn't from their Bible-based studies. I don't know how long this will be allowed (I'm guessing that over time the government will want more say over curriculum and where the money goes), but creative families are enjoying this opportunity while they have it.

Second, for kids who are serious about certain sports or other activities (such as band or theater), charter schools are sometimes the very best option—even if they are a compromise—because kids who are enrolled in a charter school can legally participate in school activities. This is especially important for kids who want to pursue these activities beyond high school.

Third, charter schools typically provide a laptop or tablet for students to use, as well as funding for curriculum (and some of that funding can pay for activities and outside classes if they fall under the "school" category). This can be a game changer for families on a tight budget.

Charter schools began in the 1990s, and they are growing in popularity each year, with many having long waiting lists to get in. Some charter schools are run much like a conventional school, with students attending class in person. These are often referred to as "choice schools" because they offer a unique focus or some innovative teaching method. For instance, there are STEM-focused charter schools and charter schools held outdoors that teach a nature-focused curriculum.

Here in Hawaii and in some other states and districts, most charter schools are run as distance-learning programs. Students may meet with the teacher for part of or a whole school day once or twice a week, and then spend the rest of the time at home. The charter school provides the curriculum, and a teacher is available to provide extra help or answer questions.

Some states also have charter schools that allow parents to choose their child's curriculum. I have friends in California who purchase homeschool curriculum using the charter school funding and only have to turn in a monthly sample of their kids' work to the charter school teacher. The schoolwork they turn in cannot be faith-based, so that limits their curriculum options, but it does allow them to do Bible class on the side (without an expectation for credits). Thus far, these families have been very happy to receive in the range of $2,000 to $3,000 a year per student, along with a tablet. Their kids also have the option to participate in public school sports or other extracurricular activities.

As you can see, there are some true perks to having your child attend a charter school. Some parents who feel overwhelmed by the idea of independent homeschooling are drawn to charter schools, and I understand why.

However, from my experience and the research I have done, I would encourage families to at least consider if homeschooling independently might actually be your best option. You will likely be surprised to realize that it is not as difficult as you'd imagine it would be, and there is great satisfaction in giving your kids the education you want—and the education *they* want—without depending on the government for any of it.

## Hybrid Schools

Hybrid schooling, also sometimes referred to as blended learning or hybrid homeschooling, is exactly what it sounds like: a mix of learning in-person at a brick-and-mortar school and doing school from home. Some public schools offer hybrid options, and some private schools do as well. Hybrid schooling does have some benefits:

- Curriculum and courses are usually set, leaving fewer decisions for parents who don't feel comfortable creating their own plan.
- Students can benefit from involvement in public school sports and other extracurricular activities.

- Students spend much time at home, or at least more than they would if they attended an in-person school full-time.
- Students get to see school friends regularly.
- Students are able to experience two different school environments, which may keep learning interesting.
- Students interact with both their parents and outside teachers, which may better prepare them for college classes.

But hybrid schooling also has some challenges:

- Parents have less control over curriculum choices and the schedule. (Also, if it is a public school, the curriculum will be secular.)
- Students will be required to be connected to technology for much of their communication.
- Students will be expected to follow public school rules and regulations related to testing, timelines, etc.
- Private hybrid schools are often expensive.
- Hybrid schooling takes away the flexibility of homeschooling, such as being able to travel whenever you want or study what you want when you want.
- Students are prevented from working at their own pace, and study time can bleed outside of "normal" school hours if a student falls behind.

Notice that some of the pros and cons are the same, which points to the importance of knowing what your family needs and values. If choosing a curriculum is important to you, then a hybrid model will not be ideal; if you don't want the pressure of choosing a curriculum, then it may be a good option. You'll want to weigh the pros and cons for your family in light of the options available to you before making a decision about this type of schooling.

Since public schools in Hawaii don't offer hybrid options, and we don't live near private schools that might be an option, we have never investigated using a hybrid model with our sons. Though it hasn't been easy, I have loved the experience and simplicity of having my sons do all their schooling at home

> Resist FOMO and comparison. You have your own story. It won't look like anyone else's. And that's ok!

(using many online courses). However, I do understand where a hybrid model could be a blessing for various family situations, and I encourage every family to choose what is best for them.

With so many options for families, my greatest advice is to pray, ask questions of people you respect in your community, and consider what would be the best fit for your family considering your specific circumstances and values. Resist FOMO and comparison. You have your own story. It won't look like anyone else's. And that's ok! Embrace it and enjoy it, knowing that whatever path you choose, it will come and go more quickly than you could ever imagine. So make the most of the time you have and do what's best for your family.

## TAKE-HOME THOUGHT

Instead of being overwhelmed by the educational options, we can be grateful to have options! And keep in mind, our greatest calling as parents is to "bring them up in the training and instruction of the Lord" (Ephesians 6:4).

## REFLECTION QUESTION

In light of your family's circumstances and your parenting goals, which schooling option seems to be the best fit for you in this season?

## CHAPTER 13

# A DAY IN THE LIFE

## Homeschool Schedules

One of the first questions I get from homeschool-curious people is "What does your (homeschool) day look like?" Especially if I get caught at the beach or the grocery store on a Tuesday morning with kids in tow, people want to know, "How does this homeschooling thing actually work?" *I get it.* For those of us raised in a traditional school, it can be hard to imagine how a family might get through multiple subjects with multiple kids in one smallish house with all the other things that go on in a normal day at home (hello, dog, cat, laundry, errands, phone calls, and a million other distractions!).

Along with just about every other part of homeschooling, schedules will be unique for each family (and often for each child). But seeing a sample schedule (or a few of them) can be helpful when becoming homeschoolers. This chapter provides such an example, and I also have included in the resource section a link to additional homeschool schedules of other families.

## Start with the Bigger Picture: Your Yearly Schedule

The first question you'll want to consider is whether you want to follow a typical school-year calendar or do your own thing. (Yes, you get to choose!) Many families find year-round homeschooling to be best (with nice breaks included throughout the year). Another idea I love is using a four-day school week. There are currently no laws that tell families which days or times they must do school. You have freedom to make a plan that works for you.

You'll find a yearlong calendar template in the resource section, which is a great way to map out a loose plan for your year. If you pencil in numbered school days (and I do mean pencil, because I typically erase and make changes throughout the year) and fit in around 180 days by the end of the school year, you are off to a great start! Don't forget to include those much-needed breaks and even a few random days off, which give you margin to catch up or get to the dentist or take a field trip (or take a sick day, if you must). When we hit the winter doldrums or get envious of the social media images we see of snow days, our family has been known to take a "snow day" just to watch a movie (an educational one, of course—wink, wink), bake something yummy, or head out on an adventure. Yay for homeschooling!

## Next, Create a "School Day" Plan

Just to get you started thinking about things, here is a very simple example of a daily homeschool routine for a family with middle school kids:

7:30 a.m. | Wake up, breakfast, devotions, chores
9:00 a.m. | Bible lesson
9:30 a.m. | Math

10:15 a.m. | Break

10:30 a.m. | Language arts (depending on age may include
spelling, literature, handwriting, etc.)

11:30 a.m. | Science

12:30 p.m. | Lunch + recess/free time for nonscreen activities

1:30 p.m. | History or social studies

2:00 p.m. | Reading/Projects/Electives/Sports

Our family has followed a schedule like this at various times, but more recently Levi has preferred a broader to-do list of subjects that need to get done by the end of the day or even the end of the week. He checks items off the list as he completes them, with the goal of fitting everything into a four-day school week. He spends a lot of his time working out (training for the PGA is no joke, haha), hitting golf balls in the yard, or exploring the outdoors with our dog. This means that a four-hour school day sometimes takes eight hours—but that is his choice!

Here's an example of a seventh-grade school week checklist for Levi (which I sometimes print out and sometimes just jot down on a piece of paper):

| | Monday | Tuesday | Wednesday | Thursday | Friday |
|---|---|---|---|---|---|
| Devotions + Breakfast + Chores (daily) | | | | | |
| Math (4x weekly) | | | | | |
| IEW (writing class) (3x weekly) | | | | | |
| Grammar (4x weekly) | | | | | |
| Science (4x weekly) | | | | | |
| History (4x weekly) | | | | | |
| Piano (20 minutes/day) | | | | | |
| Worldview (3x weekly) | | | | | |
| Read (45 minutes daily) | | | | | |

| Laundry | | | | | |
|---|---|---|---|---|---|
| Write thank-you notes (by end of the week) | | | | | |

As you can see, no times are specified on this list, though some days Levi and I do try to time-block his work. (This is helpful when we need to be out the door by a certain time for golf practice or another commitment.) You will also see that I included laundry and thank-you notes on the list. Laundry is not necessarily part of school, but on certain days Levi does his own laundry, so I included it on his list that day. He also had a golf tournament coming up, and thank-you cards are required for the tournament hosts, so I added that to his schedule as well. You'll also see that most of Levi's classes must be done only three or four times a week, so if he is efficient with his time and completes everything, we can plan on a Friday off for a field trip, chores, or errands.

Some of the items on the list might take thirty to forty-five minutes (math and IEW, for example), while devotions, chores, or worldview might take only fifteen to twenty minutes. Levi often splits up his reading time throughout the day, reading for fifteen minutes two times during the day and then for another fifteen minutes at bedtime.

I also try to start the week by looking at what needs to get done over the whole week, then sit down with Levi to plan out the schedule. Since he is a serious golfer, there are some days that we both know he will not get a lot of schoolwork done. That is okay, but it means he might need to double up on other days by knocking out more than one lesson or reading ahead. Honestly, Levi's schedule looks a lot like my own to-do list. And that is real life, right?

Many schedule templates and homeschool planners are available and can be very helpful. I've never claimed expertise in time management or scheduling, but I am planning to use a homeschool planner as we begin to organize and track Levi's high school years.

Before we move on, here are a few more things to keep in mind as you plan your schedule:

1. **Plan margin in your day and week.** Things always take longer than you expect, and bathroom, snack, and fresh-air breaks are really important.

2. **Stay flexible.** When the repairman comes and has to turn off the electricity, Grandma stops by to say hi, or the pro surf contest is going on and we "have to watch," I always remind myself, "This is why we homeschool." It's okay to get off schedule, take a little longer, or put off a class until the evening (or the next day). Flexibility is key, and a rigid schedule will ruin everyone's homeschool experience.

3. **Mornings are the best.** I have often ~~complained~~ noted that it's too bad mornings are truly the best *for everything*. They are the best time to do devotions, to exercise, to focus on a hard subject, to get work done, and everything else. But this means we need to maximize our mornings, which also means we need to go to bed at a decent hour. This is not easy for my family, and we are a (never-ending) work in progress. But the bottom line is this: a good morning will set the tone for the rest of the day, and a good morning starts the night before. So we should all be wise with our time.

4. **Don't be afraid to experiment.** You might think you hate a firm schedule, but once you try it, you won't believe how freeing it is. You might think that every day has to start with math, but actually your child does math better in the afternoon. A little exercise in the morning or a nap after lunch might be the secret to a better day. Trying a variety of approaches is the best way to find what works for everyone.

**5. Don't forget the little things.** This isn't necessarily schedule-related, but I think it fits here. Some of the things that add exponentially to our school day are very simple: Lighting a scented candle. Playing quiet jazz or classical music. Turning on the AC when it's hot. (We dream of a fireplace in the winter here, so if you have one, enjoy it on our behalf!) Sipping hot cider or baking cookies in the middle of the day. Snuggling on the sofa for reading time, or sprawling out on a blanket in the yard to finish a spelling list. Friends, this is the good stuff of homeschooling. Adding some comforting routines that ignite our senses always makes everything better.

## A Day in the Life When My Boys Were Ages 17, 15, 13, and 6

When all the boys were at home, daily life was very full—and sometimes a bit overwhelming. It helped greatly that my two oldest boys were mostly self-directed, but we had many schedules and activities happening at once, so I recall taking many deep breaths and reminding myself to focus on God's blessings each day.

To give you some background into our family dynamic, my husband is a hospital physician and typically works two weeks straight (every day, approximately 7:00 a.m. to 3:00 or 4:00 p.m.), followed by two weeks off (when he typically picks up some extra shifts but is home many days). He is an amazing dad and is very involved with the boys' lives, but during his days off, he also takes care of our two acres, growing fruit, cutting grass, and doing a lot of yard work. (He's our home's fix-it man as well; thank you YouTube for all the training!) I'm super blessed, but with all those responsibilities, Dave has not typically done a lot of homeschooling, cooking, or cleaning inside the house. (Call us old-fashioned—it's okay.)

Most mornings Josiah and Jonah were up by 7:00 a.m., doing

their devotions, grabbing a bowl of cereal, and beginning their school day. I made a hot breakfast a couple of times a week, but the boys were expected to serve themselves otherwise. Luke was surfing competitively at this point, so he was often out the door at sunup to surf. If my husband was off work, he would drive Luke to the beach and film his surfing, and sometimes the older brothers might join him as well. If Dave was away at work, Josiah or a friend would drive Luke to the beach in the morning. If this wasn't an option, Luke would just do school all morning and wait to surf later in the day. On those days, he, too, would start with devotions and breakfast before diving into his school day.

I tried to be up around 6:00 a.m., doing my devotions and sometimes squeezing in a thirty-minute run or workout in the garage before I started the school day. (I aim for getting exercise four days a week, and daily Bible devotions are nonnegotiable for me.) Levi would wake up between 7:30 and 8:00 a.m., and I'd read to him from a kid's devotional, then fix him his breakfast.

The older boys did most of their school day independently. Most of the time, all three older boys began their school day with an Abeka Bible video. They would watch the video, sometimes listening while they made their beds or fiddled with something. But they all enjoyed learning about the Bible, and they really enjoyed their online teachers. I'm pretty sure they have emailed a number of them and guaranteed they would all name Mr. McBride as a virtual mentor who helped to shape their values as teenagers. (If someone out there knows Mr. McBride personally, please let him know!)

From there everyone moved at their own pace. The boys each had a list of daily class assignments that needed to be done, and they tackled them one at a time. They didn't finish all their schoolwork every day, nor did they finish every curriculum every year. But I checked in often, encouraging them to stay on schedule with the hope of seeing them finish their curriculum by the end of each

May. Throughout the day, I rotated among kids, checking on their work and delivering a smoothie or hot cider (feeding and serving my kids is my love language). I was mindful about creating a cozy, study-friendly environment with candles and soft background music.

We had an area of the house dedicated to school, but the boys tended to move their studies to their own desks or did their work in different areas of the house. We have generally tried to follow a "no screens in the bedroom" rule, but with homeschooling I found that during the day it was often best for the boys to watch their school videos at their desks in their bedrooms. When they had a video on, we simply kept the door open and I popped in often. Also, with internet filters installed on our computers, I was not as concerned that something would show up unexpectedly.

Levi used the Abeka curriculum for most of his elementary school years. This included video lessons plus workbooks. Though we often skipped the videos (I could go over the concepts with him quickly), sometimes it was helpful to have him watch a lesson on video while I worked with his older brothers, checked my email, or threw in a load of laundry. Levi also filled in time playing with Legos and toy cars, coloring, or following his dad around our property.

I love to work in the kitchen, and I frequently used to post recipes on my blog, so often while everyone was doing school, I would be making muffins or banana bread or cookies. We grow our own fruit, so I would also often dehydrate bananas or cut up mangoes or dragon fruit to freeze for future smoothies. When everyone was busy (or during seasons when I hired a helper to work with Levi for a few hours a week), I might also hop on my laptop and work on a blog post or respond to emails. Over the years my "work" life has gotten much busier, and no doubt—multitasking is key if you are a working homeschool parent!

By noon, everyone was starving (and for more than a muffin). I have always tried to make extra servings of dinner at night so I can heat up leftovers for the boys the next day. If I didn't have leftovers to serve, I might make tuna melts, a pot of mac and cheese, or a round of PB&Js. I have always tried to have some cut-up fresh veggies on hand to serve with lunch as well. Sometimes I'd have my boys make lunch, and I'd slip off for a fifteen-minute power nap.

At lunchtime we typically sat around the kitchen counter together, and the boys chatted about funny things from school, the surf, or what they were looking forward to doing later that day. I kept a stack of books near the kitchen, and while the boys ate, I read them a poem, covered an era of art or music history, or read a couple of Aesop's fables. I kept these readings short and sweet, but it felt enriching and special to do this with all the brothers together. At various times we also worked on memory verses as a family, so lunch was a great time to practice and quiz one another.

After lunch I encouraged the boys to get some fresh air. They would often hit our skate bowl, play a game of Ping-Pong, or shoot hoops outside—anything to burn off some steam before finishing their school day. I would clean up the kitchen, throw in a load of laundry, or make a phone call during that time.

By 1:00 p.m., everyone was back to school. I might try to get Levi to "rest" for a bit, but that was often a struggle. (He has major FOMO.) Often, I would lure him with a good read-aloud, which most often led to *me* dozing off—and only sometimes he would fall asleep as well. The older boys would continue their school days in the afternoon—watching school videos, doing bookwork, completing assignments, and taking quizzes or tests. Throughout the afternoon, I would rotate among kids, checking their work, giving a back scratch, or chatting about what they were learning. There was never *not* something to do.

If Dave was home on these school days, he was typically

working on the property. (Sometimes I'd send the boys out to help him, but that happened more after school hours.) When Dave had medical notes to complete, he sometimes worked alongside the boys.

On his workdays, Dave could usually be home by 3:30 or 4:00 p.m., and by then all the older boys were ready to hit the beach (unless they had youth group or work or some other activity that day). Sometimes I would join them (and I never regretted an afternoon at the beach!), most of the time I took advantage of having the house to myself for a couple of hours (*sigh*). That was when I would bust out a blog post, update my social media, and work on growing my writing career. By 6:00 p.m. I would start dinner.

The guys would get home from their activities between between 6:00 and 7:00. (as the sun went down). Most nights we sat down to dinner together, followed by playing a game, watching a TV show, or having a family Ping-Pong tournament. We also aimed to do family devotions when we could. Sometimes we went through a family devotional book, other times we read a few verses from the Bible, and then Dave or Jonah would lead us in a few worship songs on the guitar. We'd close with prayer. This all took fifteen to thirty minutes, and though they didn't happen super consistently, these are some of our favorite family memories.

The older boys often had extra reading to do from their school day before bed, and Luke often had surf video to edit and post on social media. We have intended to get on an earlier bedtime routine as a family ever since I can remember, but I think we all enjoyed our cozy evening activities.

As with all families, many aspects of our "day in the life" changed through the seasons. The older boys had youth group at least one night a week, and as they neared college age, they also worked at a restaurant and attended other Bible studies and social gatherings. Dave and I tried to fit in a date night at least every other week. (The boys loved their "bro nights" when we went out.) Homeschooling changed over the years as well, and now that Levi is my only homeschool student, it continues to shift. But I am glad to know that the freedom to change things up is much of the beauty of homeschooling.

Note: The resource section includes a link to "A Day in the Life" bonus chapter, which is a collection of day-in-the-life schedules from other homeschool families. From homeschooling a houseful to homeschooling an only child, from following an organized curriculum to learning in a more free-flow manner, from homeschooling special needs kids to homeschooling with a newborn in the home—you'll find a little bit of everything there!

## TAKE-HOME THOUGHT

Homeschoolers have the benefit of being as structured or flexible with their days as they need to be, in the season they are in.

## REFLECTION QUESTION

What are some of your greatest priorities when it comes to scheduling your days? How might homeschooling support what you value the most?

# THE FINAL NUDGE

## Aka "The Most Important Chapter"

I'm writing this final chapter the day after attending a wedding with my husband. It was a beautiful oceanfront ceremony for a fellow doctor and his bride, and during the reception we were seated at a table full of physicians. Over small talk, an internal medicine doctor asked me what I do for work, which is always challenging to answer.

"Mostly," I began, "I'm a homeschool mom." I paused, planning to go on to say that I am also a podcaster and an author and . . .

But I didn't get any further because the doctor broke in with an enthusiastic, "Oh, wow! That is fantastic! So important! I have so much respect for homeschooling. But I could *never* do that!"

I looked at this man and smiled. *He's a doctor, for heaven's sake,* I thought. *Does he realize how many years he went to school to do what he does every day? Does he remember how hard that was?*

Of course, I always assume that people are just being nice or covering whatever their true thoughts are about homeschooling when they say something like that, but this guy seemed sincere.

He noted how impressed he's been with homeschool families, then he went on to share some of his honest thoughts on the state of our culture, and how I'm making a difference in the next generation and in the world.

Then he repeated, slowly and clearly, "But I . . . could *never* do it," with such emphasis you would have thought I was asking him to homeschool my children.

I gave up on my idea of impressing him with my podcasting and writing skills, since I clearly had already won this guy's respect.

The man who identifies life-threatening infections and revives people in cardiac arrest was intent on my knowing that he could never do what I do. I've had other people tell me, "I could never do that," but perhaps because I was preparing to write this closing chapter, the words hit me differently this time.

Instead of shaking my head or laughing it off (although it is kind of funny, you must agree), I decided to take his words to heart.

And as Dave drove us home last night, I repeated the man's words to myself (and ok, out loud to Dave too!).

*I am a homeschool mom.*

It's a job that not everyone can do (or is willing to try).

What I do impacts lives . . . families . . . generations!

It may (or may not) be harder than being a doctor. (I'm still not convinced.) But yes, it's a big deal.

It's good to note that many great men and women of history were homeschooled. We can look back at our country's presidents, including George Washington, Thomas Jefferson, James Madison, Abraham Lincoln, and Woodrow Wilson, who were all home-schooled. Or we can consider creative geniuses like Leonardo da Vinci, Claude Monet, Orville and Wilbur Wright, and Robert Frost. Add to the list C. S. Lewis, Louis Armstrong, Susan B. Anthony, Frank Lloyd Wright, and Albert Einstein. You may know that Mark Twain, Helen Keller, Wolfgang Amadeus Mozart, and Andrew

Carnegie were homeschooled as well as Noah Webster, Florence Nightingale, and Booker T. Washington. Though there are so many more, a few contemporary names like Condoleezza Rice, Tim Tebow, Bethany Hamilton, Ryan Gosling, and the Jonas Brothers are all on the list of famous homeschoolers.[1]

You may have already heard the story of Thomas Edison's homeschool journey, but I'd like to reflect on it briefly. Thomas Edison, known as the world's greatest inventor, originally attended school in a traditional one-room schoolhouse. He was performing poorly, and legend has it his teacher sent him home one day with a note to his mother suggesting that his brains were "addled." Now, we don't use that word very much anymore, but clearly, it was not a compliment. When Edison saw his mother read the note (with tears in her eyes), he asked her what it said, and she replied that his teacher suggested he was much too gifted to be in the classroom and it would be better for her to school him at home.

Thomas Edison's mother recognized that her son perceived the world differently from his peers, and she took it upon herself to offer him a home education that would better suit his needs. From the Edison Muckers website, we read this:

> Nancy Edison encouraged her son to have both a head and hands approach to learning, allowing him to have his own laboratory in their small basement—a place where his father became quite concerned as various small explosions emanated, along with strange smells. Nancy endured over dad's protests and imbued Tom with four life-long pillars of learning:
>
> 1. Do not be afraid to fail, keep trying, learn from your mistakes
> 2. Read across the entire span of literature, not just what you like

3. It is OK to work with your hands and learn from life,
   not all important things come from books
4. Never stop learning, keep improving yourself.[2]

Some have questioned if this story is entirely true, but it is entirely believable because countless mothers do exactly what Nancy Edison did for the exceptionally gifted, uniquely challenged, amazing-in-a-million-different-ways kids in their care every day. This is the heart of a homeschooling parent. (I love that Edison's dad was concerned but allowed his son to continue learning at home!) I cannot help but wonder how different our world might be today if Edison's mom had not chosen to embrace her son's unique gifts and homeschool him accordingly.

If, after reading this book, you are still on the fence about homeschooling, my greatest suggestion for you is to take time to pray about it. The Bible contains no commands specifically telling us to homeschool our kids, but we do know that Scripture is clear about a parent's responsibility in raising their children. A few verses we have already reflected on in this book:

> Train up a child in the way he should go;
>> even when he is old he will not depart from it.
>> (Proverbs 22:6 ESV)

Bring them up in the discipline and instruction of the Lord.
(Ephesians 6:4 ESV)

Teach [these words of mine] to your children, talking about them when you sit at home and when you walk along the road, when you lie down and when you get up. (Deuteronomy 11:19)

And my favorite verse for parenting motivation:

I have no greater joy than to hear that my children are walking in truth. (3 John 1:4)

My parenting journey is far from over, but from the little experience I have with three grown children, I can tell you that this final verse resonates deeply with me. The joy I experience from hearing that each of my boys is walking in God's Truth exceeds any other joy I have known. And it makes any sacrifice I have made for them so very worthwhile!

> The joy I experience from hearing that each of my boys is walking in God's Truth exceeds any other joy I have known.

## Where to Go from Here

We have covered a lot in this book, and I do hope that it can be both a guidebook and a resource for you. Perhaps you will return to certain chapters over time as your kids grow up. It is my hope that I've communicated as a good friend or caring big sister, walking with you through your homeschool journey no matter when or where you choose to start.

I am aware that some of you will read this book and decide that homeschooling is not for you. You might be realizing that the sacrifice is just too much in this season you are in. Or that your obstacles are not going to budge. Perhaps you already have a situation that you feel good about and you're going to stick with it. Whatever your reason, I'm cheering for you every step of the way. God knows you, your kids, and every detail of your lives, and he will be there to help you as you do your best to raise your children with intention. (I will be too!)

To those of you who are already homeschooling or are ready to take the leap and try it, I am so very proud of you. Parenting is a

> Parenting is a huge sacrifice, and homeschooling is even more sacrifice. Be assured that God will give you everything you need to fulfill his calling in your life.

huge sacrifice, and homeschooling is even more sacrifice. Be assured that God will give you everything you need to fulfill his calling in your life.

As we wrap up, I hope you'll take full advantage of the resource section. I have a lot of great stuff there for you! You'll also find a link there for a brand-new online course I created that should be the perfect next step for you to take after reading this book. (I'm so excited! I hope you'll hurry over and check that out right away.)

Of course you can also always track me down on my website: monicaswanson.com. I hope to get to know you more, and I promise I'll be praying for you!

Now I'm imagining sitting across the table from you, steaming coffee in front of us, as I look into your eyes and say, "I know you can do this! Here's to all the good, hard, and beautiful adventures you'll have as you are *becoming homeschoolers*. I can't wait to hear about your journey!"

# BECOMING HOMESCHOOLERS RESOURCES

Below you will find a list of all resources mentioned in *Becoming Homeschoolers*. Because most of the resources are found on the internet, and so that I can keep things up to date over time, you can use the following link to access everything on my website, here:

**www.monicaswanson.com/bh-resources**

## Chapter-by-Chapter Bonus Resources:

### Chapter 3

Bonus chapter: "Practical Help for Real Homeschool Challenges"
Homeschool resources for single parents

### Chapter 4

Legal guidelines for homeschooling for each state
Other helpful HSLDA pages
Book: *103 Top Homeschool Picks* by Cathy Duffy
Website with Cathy's Top Picks
Favorite homeschool curriculums by grade level
List of homeschool planners
List of homeschool communities and conventions

## Chapter 5

My (online) Character Training Course (such a great fit for
homeschool families!)

## Chapter 6

Favorite read-aloud books by age level

## Chapter 7

Standardized testing requirements by state
List of electives to consider
A printable prayer and Bible journaling template for kids

## Chapter 8

Graduation requirements for public schools
Sample homeschool high school plan
Resources to help with the high school planning process
Sample school year plan

## Chapter 9

List of post–high school career possibilities
Resources for offering standardized tests at home
College Board website with information about testing options
and advanced placement classes and credits
CLEP test, DSST and UEXcel test information
Transcript-creation services and sites that offer help with
creating a high school transcript
Information about filling out the Common Application for
colleges

## Chapter 13

Yearlong homeschool calendar template
Bonus chapter: "A Day in the Life" from a variety of homeschool
families

## Chapter 14

My (online) Homeschool Course (the best next step after
reading this book!)

# ACKNOWLEDGMENTS

First and foremost, thank you, God, for the gift of family and your grand design for passing on truth from one generation to the next. Thank you for the gift of children and for trusting us to raise them! Thank you especially for the grace and mercy that have covered over a multitude of our mistakes and sins. You are the perfect Father, Teacher, and Friend. I can't wait to keep learning and growing with you for an eternity!

Thank you to my blog and book readers, podcast listeners, and anyone kind enough to spend a few minutes on my social media accounts. You have encouraged me, challenged me, and inspired me to provide a meaningful resource for parents who want the best for their kids.

To my husband, Dave, who said yes to homeschooling, even though he thought it might make our kids weird(er). Thank you, Dave, for giving me space to feel like a horrible homeschooler, for assuring me I wasn't that bad, then to grow and get better, and then for joining me in the journey of writing a book about it!

To my four sons—Josiah, Jonah, Luke, and Levi: What an absolute joy it has been to be not only your mom but your primary teacher. Oh my goodness, I am the most blessed! (Levi, we are not done yet, but let's enjoy the rest of our adventure together!) I have loved homeschooling all of you.

To my parents: Thank you for believing in me and always supporting our family and my work. You may not have homeschooled me, but you have taught me more than anyone else!

To my agent, Alex Field, you and your team at the Bindery Agency have been so good to me. I feel honored to work with you!

To the team at Zondervan, thank you so much for trusting me with a second book! I loved working with you on *Raising Amazing* and was thrilled to get another chance to team up. Carolyn McCready, it was *you* who jotted that note in the margin of the *Raising Amazing* manuscript, suggesting that my "next book" might be one about homeschooling. Thank you for writing the words that lit my heart on fire for this book.

Janna Walkup, thank you so much for saying yes to partnering to do the edits on this book. Your experience as a homeschool mom added so much heart and soul to this book. Kim Tanner, thank you for all your work on the final manuscript. I can't imagine where it would be without you! Katie Painter, your hard work and dedication are extraordinary, and your positivity always puts me at ease. You have made the publishing process so enjoyable (twice!). Matt Bray, you're a genius, and I am aware that you do more than I even know (or could understand!). Meaghan Minkus, you've graciously helped with so many details of this project. Thank you! And to the rest of the team at Zondervan (there are so many!)—I appreciate you all very much.

Also, to those friends who said yes to reading chapters or sharing your "day in the life" or just listening to me process this book: Gisele McDaniel, your "friend edits" and feedback were so valuable, once again! Tama Fortner, you were so kind to look at early chapters for me. And Jen Gray, thank you for speed-reading chapters and always encouraging me.

Finally, thank you to the multitude of friends, mentors, and prayer warriors who have supported me in my homeschool journey as well as in my writing career. To name just a few: Judy Huf, Berit Kawaguchi, Emily Turner, Tiffany Jaeger, Wendy Speake, Rebecca Jenkins, Jessica Smartt, Leanne Benson, and many others. I am forever grateful to each of you!

# NOTES

### How We Became Homeschoolers

1. Peter Jamison, Laura Meckler, Prayag Gordy, Clara Ence Morse, and Chris Alcantara, "Homeschooling Growth Data by District," October 31, 2023, https://www.washingtonpost.com/education/interactive/2023/homeschooling-growth-data-by-district/.

### Chapter 1: The Life They'll Thank You for Later (Part 1)

1. Lisa M. Treleaven, "Quantitative Insights into the Academic Outcomes of Homeschools from the Classic Learning Test," *Home School Researcher* 38, no. 1 (2022): 1–13, https://www.nheri.org/wp-content/uploads/2022/12/HSR381-Treleaven-article-only.pdf.
2. Allison Slater Tate, "Colleges Welcome a Growing Number of Homeschool Students," NBC News, February 17, 2016, https://www.nbcnews.com/feature/college-game-plan/colleges-welcome-growing-number-homeschooled-students-n520126.
3. Sofia W. Tong and Idil Tuysuzoglu, "From Homeschool to Harvard," *Crimson*, December 10, 2017, https://www.thecrimson.com/article/2017/12/10/homeschool-harvard/.
4. Laura Meckler and Peter Jamison, "Takeaways from Homeschooling Enrollment Poll," *Washington Post*, October 31, 2023, https://www.washingtonpost.com/education/2023/10/31/takeaways-homeschooling-enrollment-poll.
5. George Amos Dorsey, Quotefancy, accessed October 17, 2023, https://quotefancy.com/quote/1603136/George-Amos-Dorsey-Good-honest-hardheaded-character-is-a-function-of-the-home-If-the.
6. "Teens and Social Media Use: What's the Impact," Mayo Clinic, February 26, 2022, https://www.mayoclinic.org/healthy-lifestyle/tween-and-teen-health/in-depth/teens-and-social-media-use/art-20474437.

7. "Study: Homeschooled Kids Sleep More Than Others," *Behavioral Sleep Medicine*, March 2, 2016, https://www.eurekalert.org/news-releases /812502.

8. Jessica Smartt, *Let Them Be Kids: Adventure, Boredom, Innocence, and Other Gifts Children Need* (Nashville: Thomas Nelson, 2020), 21.

9. Michelle Cardel, Amanda L. Willig, Akilah Dulin-Keita, et al., "Home-Schooled Children Are Thinner, Leaner, and Report Better Diets Relative to Traditionally-Schooled Children," NIH National Library of Medicine, https://www.ncbi.nlm.nih.gov /pmc/articles/PMC3946420/. Published in final edited form in *Obesity* (Silver Spring) 22, no. 2 (February 2014): 497–503.

10. Brian D. Ray, "Research Facts on Homeschooling," NHERI, rev. July 20, 2023, https://www.nheri.org/research-facts-on-homeschooling/; John Wesley Taylor V, "Self-Concept in Home-Schooling Children" (diss. 726), Digital Commons @ Andrews University, 1986, https:// digitalcommons.andrews.edu/cgi /viewcontent.cgi?article=1725&context=dissertations.

11. Thomas C. Smedley, "Socialization of Home School Children—a Communication Approach" (master's thesis, Radford University, May 1992), http://myplace.frontier.com/~thomas.smedley /smedleys.htm.

## Chapter 2: The Life They'll Thank You for Later (Part 2)

1. Laura Meckler, Peter Jamison, Emily Guskin, and Scott Clement, "Home Schooling Today Is Less Religious and More Diverse, Poll Finds," *Washington Post*, December 18, 2023, https://www .washingtonpost.com/education/2023/09/26/home-schooling-vs -public-school-poll/.

2. John Woodrow Cox, Stephen Rich, Linda Chong, Lucas Trevor, John Muyskens, and Monica Ulmanu, "There Have Been 394 School Shootings since Columbine," *Washington Post,* April 3, 2023, https:// www.washingtonpost.com/education/interactive/school-shootings -database/.

3. "Bulletproof Backpacks, Homeschool: With No New Gun Laws, Parents Make Changes of Their Own," NBC News, June 12, 2022, https://www .nbcnews.com/news/us-news/uvalde-shooting-parents-feel-no-safe -place-children-rcna32534.

4. Bruce Simons-Morton and Tilda Farhat, "Recent Findings on Peer Group Influences on Adolescent Substance Use," *Journal of Primary Prevention* 31, no. 4 (August 2010): 191–208, NIH National Library of

Medicine, https://www.ncbi.nlm.nih.gov /pmc/articles/PMC3313483/.

5. Michael G. Vaughn, Christopher P. Salas-Wright, Kristen P. Kremer, et al., "Are Homeschooled Adolescents Less Likely to Use Alcohol, Tobacco, and Other Drugs?," *Drug and Alcohol Dependence* 155 (October 2015): 97–104, NIH National Library of Medicine, https://www.ncbi.nlm.nih.gov /pmc/articles/PMC4652803/.

6. Vaughn et al., "Are Homeschooled Adolescents."

7. "States That Don't Teach Evolution," World Population Review, updated August 2023, https://worldpopulationreview.com/state-rankings/states -that-dont-teach-evolution.

8. Zach Goldberg and Eric Kaufmann, "Yes, Critical Race Theory Is Being Taught in Schools," *City Journal*, October 20, 2022, https://www.city -journal.org/yes-critical-race-theory-is-being-taught-in-schools.

9. Katie J. M. Baker, "When Students Change Gender Identity, and Parents Don't Know," *New York Times*, January 22, 2023, https://www.nytimes .com/2023/01/22/us/gender-identity-students-parents.html.

10. Tony Evans, "America's Racial Crisis Is a Result of the Failure of the Church to Deal with Racism," *Dallas Morning News*, June 15, 2020, https://www.dallasnews.com/opinion/commentary/2020/06/15/tony -evans-americas-racial-crisis-is-a-result-of-the-failure-of-the-church -to-deal-with-racism/.

11. Monica Swanson, *Raising Amazing: Bringing Up Kids Who Love God, Like Their Family, and Do the Dishes without Being Asked* (Grand Rapids: Zondervan, 2023), 216.

## Chapter 3: Why Not?

1. Jonathan Rothwell, "Teens Spend Average of 4.8 Hours on Social Media per Day," Gallup.Com, November 21, 2023, https://news.gallup.com/ poll/512576/teens-spend-average-hours-social-media-per-day.aspx.

2. Brian D. Ray, "Research Facts on Homeschooling," NHERI, rev. July 20, 2023, https://www.nheri.org/research-facts-on-homeschooling/.

3. Dorothy L. Sayers, AZQuotes.com, accessed November 5, 2023, https:// www.azquotes.com/quote/547760.

4. Jen Mackinnon, WHM Club, accessed October 17, 2023, https:// workinghomeschoolmomclub.com.

## Chapter 4: Getting Started

1. "Books by Cathy Duffy," accessed January 12, 2024, https://cathyduffyreviews.com/books-by-cathy-duffy.
2. Charlotte Mason, AZ Quotes, accessed October 17, 2023, https://www.azquotes.com/quote/732970.
3. "What Is the Trivium? An Easy-to-Understand Analogy," Classical Conversations, October 31, 2022, https://classicalconversations.com/blog/what-is-the-trivium/.
4. "Find Your Homeschooling Method," Homeschool.com, accessed October 17, 2023, https://www.homeschool.com/homeschooling-methods/.
5. "Do I Need to Find an Accredited Homeschool Program?," Time 4 Learning, accessed October 17, 2023, https://www.time4learning.com/blog/category/tips-worksheets/do-i-need-accredited-homeschool-program/.

## Chapter 7: Awesome and Awkward

1. Monica Swanson, "What A Middle School Boy Needs Most from His Parents," Monica Swanson (blog), July 21, 2019, https://monicaswanson.com/middle-school-boy-needs/.
2. Kelly Field, "Middle School's Moment: What the Science Tells Us about Improving the Middle Grades," Hechinger Report, August 16, 2021, https://hechingerreport.org/middle-schools-moment-what-the-science-tells-us-about-improving-the-middle-grades/.

## Chapter 8: Independent and Inspired

1. "Church Dropouts Have Risen to 64%—but What about Those Who Stay?," Barna, September 4, 2019, https://www.barna.com/research/resilient-disciples/.
2. George Barna, *Revolutionary Parenting: Raising Your Kids to Be Spiritual Champions* (Carol Stream, IL: Tyndale, 2004), 31.

## Chapter 9: The Nitty-Gritty

1. "College Board - SAT, AP, College Search and Admission Tools," accessed January 12, 2024, https://www.collegeboard.org/.
2. "AP Classes: What Are They, and Why Should You Take Them?," Academic Approach, December 16, 2021, https://www.academicapproach.com/what-are-ap-classes/.
3. "AP Credit Policy Search," College Board, accessed October 17, 2023,

https://apstudents.collegeboard.org/getting-credit-placement/search
-policies.

4. Lisa Davis, "How to Navigate the Common App as a Homeschool
Parent," Fearless Homeschoolers, accessed October 17, 2023, https://
fearlesshomeschoolers.com/blog
/common-app-for-homeschoolers.

5. Melanie Hanson, "Average Student Loan Debt," Education Data
Initiative, last updated May 22, 2023, https://educationdata.org
/average-student-loan-debt, emphasis in original.

6. Melanie Hanson, "Average Student Loan Debt [2023]: By Year, Age &
More," Education Data Initiative, May 22, 2023, https://educationdata
.org/average-student-loan-debt.

7. "Augustinian Scholarship," Westmont, accessed October 17, 2023,
https://www.westmont.edu/admissions-aid/affording-college/
financial-aid/scholarships/augustinian.

8. "Augustinian Scholarship."

## Chapter 10: Beyond Core Curriculum

1. "Church Dropouts Have Risen to 64%—but What about Those Who
Stay?," Barna, September 4, 2019, https://www.barna.com
/research/resilient-disciples/.

2. "What Is Deconstruction? What Does It Mean When People Say They
Are Deconstructing Their Faith?," GotQuestions.org, accessed January
12, 2024, https://www.gotquestions.org
/deconstruction.html.

3. "6 Great Quotes about the Power of Coding," Hatch, July 11, 2017,
https://www.hatchcoding.com/post/6-great-quotes-about-the-power
-of-coding.

4. "3 Ways to Determine My Teen's High School Course Credit," HSLDA,
January 15, 2020, https://hslda.org/post/3-ways-to-determine-my
-teens-high-school-course-credit.

5. "How to Assign High School Credit for Electives," Weird, Unsocialized
Homeschoolers, accessed October 17, 2023, https://www
.weirdunsocializedhomeschoolers.com/how-to-assign-high-school
-credit-for-electives/.

6. Anamaria Lopez, "How Do Colleges Evaluate Homeschooled
Students?," CollegeVine, June 27, 2016, https://blog.collegevine.com/
how-do-colleges-evaluate-homeschooled-students/.

7. Monikah Schuschu, "A Guide to Extracurriculars for Homeschooled

Students," CollegeVine, October 19, 2016, https://blog.collegevine.com
/a-guide-to-extracurriculars-for-homeschooled-students.

### Chapter 11: Good and Healthy

1. Adekunle Sanyaolu, Chuku Okorie, Xiaohua Qi, et al., "Childhood and
   Adolescent Obesity in the United States: A Public Health Concern,"
   *Global Pediatric Health* 6 (December 1, 2019): 2333794X19891305, NIH
   National Library of Medicine, https://www.ncbi.nlm.nih.gov/pmc/
   articles/PMC6887808/.
2. Regina Guthold, Gretchen A. Stevens, Leanne M. Riley, and Fiona
   C. Bull, "Global Trends in Insufficient Physical Activity among
   Adolescents: A Pooled Analysis of 298 Population-Based Surveys with
   1.6 Million Participants," *Lancet Child and Adolescent Health* 4, no. 1
   (January 2020): 23–35, ScienceDirect, https://www.sciencedirect.com/
   science/article/pii
   /S2352464219303232?via%3Dihub.
3. Taru Manyanga, Chalchisa Abdeta, Dawn Tladi, and Rowena Naidoo,
   "Children and Teens Aren't Doing Enough Physical Activity—New
   Study Sounds a Health Warning," The Conversation, January 29, 2023,
   https://theconversation.com
   /children-and-teens-arent-doing-enough-physical-activity-new-study
   -sounds-a-health-warning-196078.

### Chapter 12: Variations on Homeschooling

1. Merriam-Webster, s.v. "homeschool," accessed October 22, 2023,
   https://www.merriam-webster.com/dictionary/homeschool.
2. "What Is a Charter School?," National Charter School Resource Center,
   accessed October 22, 2023, https://charterschoolcenter.ed.gov/what
   -charter-school.

### Chapter 14: The Final Nudge

1. "100 Famous Homeschoolers," AOP, June 22, 2015, https://www.aop
   .com/blog/100-famous-homeschoolers.
2. "Thomas Edison—Poster Child for the Home Schooled," Edison
   Muckers, accessed October 22, 2023, https://www.edisonmuckers.org/
   thomas-edison-poster-child-for-the-home-schooled/#comments.